CW00517924

First Published by
John Murray in 1825

This facsimile edition has been carefully scanned
and reprinted in the traditional manner by
THE LOST LIBRARY
5 High Street,
Glastonbury UK BA6 9DP

The LOST LIBRARY is a publishing house based in
Glastonbury, UK, dedicated to the reproduction
of important rare esoteric and scholarly texts for
the discerning reader.

Cataloguing Information
Fairy Legends
Thomas Crofton Croker

ISBN 978 1 906621 28 5

Printed by Replika Press Pvt Ltd,
Haryana, India

THE LOST
LIBRARY

FAIRY LEGENDS

AND

TRADITIONS

OF THE

SOUTH OF IRELAND.

The New Series.

EMBELLISHED WITH

NUMEROUS ENGRAVINGS, AND WOOD CUTS,

FROM DESIGNS BY BROOKE.

PUBLISHED BY

THE LOST LIBRARY

GLASTONBURY, ENGLAND

to face title page

"What's your name my darling?" says Dick

Published Decr 1st [illegible] by J Murray London

TO

SIR WALTER SCOTT, BART.

THIS VOLUME

IS INSCRIBED,

IN ADMIRATION OF HIS GENIUS,

AND

IN GRATITUDE FOR HIS KINDNESS,

BY

T. CROFTON CROKER.

The Etchings by, and Wood Engravings after the drawings of W. H. Brooke, F. S. A.

PREFACE.

In redeeming a promise made in the preface to the second edition of the Fairy Legends and Traditions of the South of Ireland, and placing before the public a second part of the same work, I trust that the indulgence which the former volume has experienced will be extended to the present collection.

The literary intercourse of European nations is now so great, and translation so common, that a writer has in general but little reason to plume himself on his work having appeared in a French or German dress. But the character of the translator may confer value on that otherwise indifferent circumstance; and I cannot but feel and express a considerable degree of satisfaction at observing my former volume translated into German by such eminent scholars as the brothers Grimm, whose friendship and valuable correspondence it has also procured me. Their version, which I had not seen when the second edition appeared, is, as might be expected, faithful and spirited; and to it they have prefixed a most learned and valuable introduction respecting Fairy superstition in general.

"Whoever," says Dr. Grimm, in the preface to the German translation, "has a relish for innocent and simple poetry, will feel attracted by these tales. They possess a peculiar flavour which is not without its charms, and they come to us from a country of which we are in general reminded in but few, and those not very pleasant relations. It is, moreover, inhabited by a people whose antiquity and early civilization is attested by history; and who, as they in part still speak their own language, must retain living traces of their former times, to show which the belief in supernatural beings here exhibited yields, perhaps, one of the best examples."

The following extracts from the public prints are evidences of the popular superstition of Ireland, and are in themselves too remarkable to be omitted in a work professing to illustrate the subject. Deeply as I lament that such delusion should exist, these facts will sufficiently prove that I have not (as has been insinuated) conjured up forgotten tales, or attempted to perpetuate a creed which had disappeared. On the contrary, my aim has been to bring the twilight tales of the peasantry before the view of the philosopher; as, if suffered to remain unnoticed, the latent belief in them may long have lingered among the inhabitants of the wild mountain and lonesome glen, to retard the progress of their civilization.

"TRALEE ASSIZES, July, 1826.—*Child Murder.*—Ann Roche, an old woman of very advanced age, was indicted for the murder of Michael Leahy, a young child, by drowning him in the Flesk. This case, which at first assumed a very serious aspect, from the meaning imputed to words spoken by the prisoner, 'that the sin of the child's death was on the grandmother, and not on the prisoner,' turned out to be a homicide committed under the delusion of the grossest superstition. The child, though four years old, could neither stand, walk, or speak—*it was thought to be fairy-struck*—and the grandmother ordered the prisoner and one of the witnesses, Mary Clifford, to bathe the child every morning in that pool of the river Flesk where the boundaries of three farms met; they had so bathed it for three mornings running, and on the last morning the prisoner kept the child longer under the water than usual, when her companion (the witness, Mary Clifford) said to the prisoner, 'How can you hope ever to see God after this?' to which the prisoner replied, 'that the sin was on the grandmother and not on her.' Upon cross-examination, the witness said it was not done with intent to kill the child, but to cure it—*to put the fairy out of it.*

"The policeman who apprehended her stated, that on charging her with drowning the child, she said it was no matter if it had died four years ago.

"Baron Pennefather said, that though it was a case of suspicion, and required to be thoroughly examined into, yet the jury would not be safe in convicting the prisoner of murder, however strong their suspicions might be. Verdict—Not guilty."—*Morning Post.*

"An inquest was held on Saturday last, on the body of a man of the name of Connor, a schoolmaster, in the neighbourhood of Castle Nenor, county of Sligo. This unfortunate man had expressed his determination to read his recantation on the following Sunday, notwithstanding all the efforts of his friends to dissuade him; they succeeded in enticing him into a house, where he was found suspended from the ceiling. A verdict of Wilful Murder against persons unknown was found at the inquest, and warrants were issued against his own father and two of his cousins on suspicion of having perpetrated the deed. These persons endeavoured to circulate a report that he had been hanged by the *fairies*. It appeared on the inquest that those persons, who were the first to give the alarm, had passed by some houses in the immediate vicinity of the house where the body was found hanging."—*Dublin Evening Mail, 18th April*, 1827.

It would be in the power of every one conversant with the manners of the country to produce instances of the undoubting belief in these superstitions, if not so formal and revolting as the foregoing, yet fully as convincing.

Notwithstanding the collection of Irish fairy legends, which I have formed in this and the former volume, the subject is far from being exhausted. But here, at least as relates to Ireland, I have determined to finish my task. A third or supplementary volume will, however, appear under the same title; and although forming a separate work on the fairy superstitions of Wales and other countries, it may be considered as illustrative of those current in Ireland.

In conclusion, I have to offer my very best acknowledgments for the many communications with which I have been favoured. To Mr. Lynch, in particular, my thanks are due for a manuscript collection of legends, from which those of "Diarmid Bawn, the Piper," and "Rent Day" have been selected. The material assistance, however, derived from various sources will be evident, and these sources are so numerous as almost to preclude individual mention.

CONTENTS.

THE MERROW.

THE DULLAHAN.

THE FIR-DARRIG.

TREASURE LEGENDS.

ROCKS AND STONES.

FAIRY LEGENDS.

THE MERROW.

———"The mysterious depths
And wild and wond'rous forms of ocean old."

THE CONCHOLOGIST.

LEGENDS OF THE MERROW.

THE LADY OF GOLLERUS.

On the shore of Smerwick harbour, one fine summer's morning, just at day-break, stood Dick Fitzgerald "shoghing the dudeen," which may be translated, smoking his pipe. The sun was gradually rising behind the lofty Brandon, the dark sea was getting green in the light, and the mists clearing away out of the valleys went rolling and curling like the smoke from the corner of Dick's mouth.

"'Tis just the pattern of a pretty morning," said Dick, taking the pipe from between his lips, and looking towards the distant ocean, which lay as still and tranquil as a tomb of polished marble. "Well, to be sure," continued he, after a pause, "'tis mighty lonesome to be talking to one's self by way of company, and not to have another soul to answer one—nothing but the child of one's own voice, the echo! I know this, that if I had the luck, or may be the misfortune," said Dick, with a melancholy smile, "to have the woman, it would not be this way with me!—and what in the wide world is a man without a wife? He's no more surely than a bottle without a drop of drink in it, or dancing without music, or the left leg of a scissars, or a fishing-line without a hook, or any other matter that is no ways complete.—Is it not so?" said Dick Fitzgerald, casting his eyes towards a rock upon the strand, which, though it could not speak, stood up as firm and looked as bold as ever Kerry witness did.

But what was his astonishment at beholding, just at the foot of that rock, a beautiful young creature combing her hair, which was of a sea-green colour; and now the salt water shining on it, appeared, in the morning light, like melted butter upon cabbage.

Dick guessed at once that she was a Merrow, although he had never seen one before, for he spied the *cohuleen driuth*, or little enchanted cap, which the sea people use for diving down into the ocean, lying upon the strand, near her; and he had heard, that if once he could possess himself of the cap, she would lose the power of going away into the water: so he seized it with all speed, and she, hearing the noise, turned her head about as natural as any Christian.

When the Merrow saw that her little diving-cap was gone, the salt tears—doubly salt, no doubt, from her—came trickling down her cheeks, and she began a low mournful cry with just the tender voice of a new-born infant. Dick, although he knew well enough what she was crying for, determined to keep the *cohuleen driuth*, let her cry never so much, to see what luck would come out of it. Yet he could not help pitying her; and when the dumb thing looked up in his face, and her cheeks all moist with tears, 'twas enough to make any one feel, let alone Dick, who had ever and always, like most of his countrymen, a mighty tender heart of his own.

"Don't cry, my darling," said Dick Fitzgerald; but the Merrow, like any bold child, only cried the more for that.

Dick sat himself down by her side, and took hold of her hand, by way of comforting her. 'Twas in no particular an ugly hand, only there was a small web between the fingers, as there is in a duck's foot; but 'twas as thin and as white as the skin between egg and shell.

"What's your name, my darling?" says Dick, thinking to make her conversant with him; but he got no answer; and he was certain sure now, either that she could not speak, or did not understand him: he therefore squeezed her hand in his, as the only way he had of talking to her. It's the universal language; and there's not a woman in the world, be she fish or lady, that does not understand it.

The Merrow did not seem much displeased at this mode of conversation; and, making an end of her whining all at once—"Man," says she, looking up in Dick Fitzgerald's face, "Man, will you eat me?"

"By all the red petticoats and check aprons between Dingle and Tralee," cried Dick, jumping up in amazement, "I'd as soon eat myself, my jewel! Is it I eat you, my pet?—Now, 'twas some ugly ill-looking thief of a fish put that notion into your own pretty head, with the nice green hair down upon it, that is so cleanly combed out this morning!"

"Man," said the Merrow, "what will you do with me, if you won't eat me?"

Dick's thoughts were running on a wife: he saw, at the first glimpse, that she was handsome; but since she spoke, and spoke too like any real woman, he was fairly in love with her. 'Twas the neat way she called him man, that settled the matter entirely.

"Fish," says Dick, trying to speak to her after her own short fashion; "fish," says he, "here 's my word, fresh and fasting, for you this blessed morning, that I 'll make you mistress Fitzgerald before all the world, and that 's what I 'll do."

"Never say the word twice," says she; "I 'm ready and willing to be yours, mister Fitzgerald; but stop, if you please, 'till I twist up my hair."

It was some time before she had settled it entirely to her liking; for she guessed, I suppose, that she was going among strangers, where she would be looked at. When that was done, the Merrow put the comb in her pocket, and then bent down her head and whispered some words to the water that was close to the foot of the rock.

Dick saw the murmur of the words upon the top of the sea, going out towards the wide ocean, just like a breath of wind rippling along, and, says he, in the greatest wonder, "Is it speaking you are, my darling, to the salt water?"

"It 's nothing else," says she, quite carelessly, "I 'm just sending word home to my father, not to be waiting breakfast for me; just to keep him from being uneasy in his mind."

"And who 's your father, my duck?" says Dick.

"What!" said the Merrow, "did you never hear of my father? he's the king of the waves, to be sure!"

"And yourself, then, is a real king's daughter?" said Dick, opening his two eyes to take a full and true survey of his wife that was to be.

"Oh, I'm nothing else but a made man with you, and a king your father;—to be sure he has all the money that's down in the bottom of the sea!"

"Money," repeated the Merrow, "what's money?"

"'Tis no bad thing to have when one wants it," replied Dick; "and may be now the fishes have the understanding to bring up whatever you bid them?"

"Oh! yes," said the Merrow, "they bring me what I want."

"To speak the truth then," said Dick, "'tis a straw bed I have at home before you, and that, I'm thinking, is no ways fitting for a king's daughter; so if 'twould not be displeasing to you, just to mention, a nice feather bed, with a pair of new blankets—but what am I talking about? may be you have not such things as beds down under the water?"

"By all means," said she, "Mr. Fitzgerald—

plenty of beds at your service. I 've fourteen oyster beds of my own, not to mention one just planting for the rearing of young ones."

"You have," says Dick, scratching his head and looking a little puzzled. "'Tis a feather bed I was speaking of—but clearly, yours is the very cut of a decent plan, to have bed and supper so handy to each other, that a person when they 'd have the one, need never ask for the other."

However, bed or no bed, money or no money, Dick Fitzgerald determined to marry the Merrow, and the Merrow had given her consent. Away they went, therefore, across the Strand, from Gollerus to Ballinrunnig, where Father Fitzgibbon happened to be that morning.

"There are two words to this bargain, Dick Fitzgerald," said his Reverence, looking mighty glum. "And is it a fishy woman you 'd marry?—the Lord preserve us!—Send the scaly creature home to her own people, that 's my advice to you, wherever she came from."

Dick had the *cohuleen driuth* in his hand, and was about to give it back to the Merrow, who looked covetously at it, but he thought for a moment, and then, says he—

"Please your Reverence, she 's a king's daughter."

"If she was the daughter of fifty kings," said

Father Fitzgibbon, "I tell you, you can't marry her, she being a fish."

"Please your Reverence," said Dick again, in an under tone, "she is as mild and as beautiful as the moon."

"If she was as mild and as beautiful as the sun, moon, and stars, all put together, I tell you, Dick Fitzgerald," said the Priest, stamping his right foot, "you can't marry her, she being a fish!"

"But she has all the gold that's down in the sea only for the asking, and I'm a made man if I marry her; and," said Dick, looking up slily, "I can make it worth any one's while to do the job."

"Oh! that alters the case entirely," replied the Priest; "why there's some reason now in what you say: why didn't you tell me this before?—marry her by all means if she was ten times a fish. Money, you know, is not to be refused in these bad times, and I may as well have the hansel of it as another, that may be would not take half the pains in counselling you that I have done."

So Father Fitzgibbon married Dick Fitzgerald to the Merrow, and like any loving couple, they returned to Gollerus well pleased with each other. Every thing prospered with Dick—he was at the sunny side of the world; the Merrow made the best of wives, and they lived together in the greatest contentment.

It was wonderful to see, considering where she had been brought up, how she would busy herself about the house, and how well she nursed the children; for, at the end of three years, there were as many young Fitzgeralds—two boys and a girl.

In short, Dick was a happy man, and so he might have continued to the end of his days, if he had only the sense to take proper care of what he had got; many another man, however, beside Dick, has not had wit enough to do that.

One day when Dick was obliged to go to Tralee, he left the wife, minding the children at home after him, and thinking she had plenty to do without disturbing his fishing tackle.

Dick was no sooner gone than Mrs. Fitzgerald set about cleaning up the house, and chancing to pull down a fishing net, what should she find behind it in a hole in the wall, but her own *cohuleen driuth.*

She took it out and looked at it, and then she thought of her father the king, and her mother the queen, and her brothers and sisters, and she felt a longing to go back to them.

She sat down on a little stool and thought over

the happy days she had spent under the sea; then she looked at her children, and thought on the love and affection of poor Dick, and how it would break his heart to lose her. "But," says she, "he won't lose me entirely, for I'll come back to him again, and who can blame me for going to see my father and my mother after being so long away from them?"

She got up and went towards the door, but came back again to look once more at the child that was sleeping in the cradle. She kissed it gently, and as she kissed it, a tear trembled for an instant in her eye and then fell on its rosy cheek. She wiped away the tear, and turning to the eldest little girl, told her to take good care of her brothers, and to be a good child herself, until she came back. The Merrow then went down to the strand.—The sea was lying calm and smooth, just heaving and glittering in the sun, and she thought she heard a faint sweet singing, inviting her to come down. All her old ideas and feelings came flooding over her mind, Dick and her children were at the instant forgotten, and placing the *cohuleen driuth* on her head, she plunged in.

Dick came home in the evening, and missing his wife, he asked Kathelin, his little girl, what had become of her mother, but she could not tell him. He then inquired of the neighbours, and he learned that she was seen going towards the strand with a strange looking thing like a cocked hat in her hand. He returned to his cabin to search for the *cohuleen driuth*. It was gone, and the truth now flashed upon him.

Year after year did Dick Fitzgerald wait expecting the return of his wife, but he never saw her more. Dick never married again, always thinking that the Merrow would sooner or later return to him, and nothing could ever persuade him but that her father the king kept her below by main force; "For," said Dick, "she surely would not of herself give up her husband and her children."

While she was with him, she was so good a wife in every respect, that to this day she is spoken of in the tradition of the country as the pattern for one, under the name of THE LADY OF GOLLERUS.

The people of Feroe say, that the seal every ninth night puts off its skin and gets a human form, and then dances and sports like the "human mortals," till it resumes its skin and becomes a seal again. It once happened that a man came by while this took place, and seeing the skin, he seized it and hid it.

When the seal, which was in the shape of a woman, could not find its skin to creep into, it was forced to remain in the human form, and, as she was fair to look upon, the same man took her to wife, had children by her, and lived right happy with her. After a long time, the wife found the skin that had been stolen and could not resist the temptation to creep into it, and so she became a seal again.

Danske Folkesagn, vol. 3. *p.* 51.

Mr. Hibbert, in his Description of the Shetland Islands, relates the same story in such a pleasing manner, that it is impossible to refrain from quoting his words. "Sometimes," he informs us, "Mermen and Merwomen have formed connubial attachments with the human race. A story is told of an inhabitant of Unst, who, in walking on the sandy margin of a voe, saw a number of these beings dancing by moonlight, and several seal-skins strewed beside them on the ground. At his approach, they immediately fled to secure their garbs, and taking upon themselves the form of seals, plunged immediately into the sea. But as the Shetlander perceived that one skin lay close to his feet, he snatched it up, bore it swiftly away, and placed it in concealment. On returning to the shore, he met the fairest damsel that was ever gazed upon by mortal eyes lamenting the robbery by which she should become an exile from her submarine friends and a tenant of the upper world. Vainly she implored the restitution of her property: the man had drunk deeply of love, and was inexorable, but offered her protection beneath his roof as his betrothed spouse. The Merlady perceiving that she must become an inhabitant of the earth, found that she could not do better than accept of the offer. This strange connubial attachment subsisted for many years, and several children were the fruits of it, who retained no farther marks of their origin, than in the resemblance which a sort of web between their fingers bore to the fore-feet of a seal—this peculiarity being possessed by the descendants of the family to the present day. The Shetlander's love for his Merwife was unbounded, but his affection was coldly returned. The lady would often steal alone to the desert strand, and, on a signal being given, a large seal would make his appearance, with whom she would hold, in an unknown tongue, an anxious conference. Years had thus glided away, when it happened that one of the children, in the course of his play, found concealed beneath a stack of corn a seal's skin, and, delighted with the prize, ran with it to his mother. Her eyes glistened with rapture—she gazed upon it as her own—as the means by which she could pass through the ocean that led to her native home. She burst forth into an ecstasy of joy, which was only moderated when she beheld her children whom she was now about to leave, and after hastily embracing them, fled with all speed towards the sea side. The husband immediately returned—learned the discovery that had taken place—ran to overtake his wife, but only arrived in time to see her transformation of shape completed—to see her in the form of a seal, bound from the ledge of a rock into the sea. The large animal of the same kind with whom she had held a secret converse soon appeared, and evidently congratulated her in the most tender manner on her escape. But before she dived to unknown depth, she cast a parting glance at the wretched Shetlander, whose despairing looks excited in her breast a few transient feelings of commiseration. 'Farewell,' said she to him: 'I loved you very well when I resided upon earth, but I always loved my first husband much better.'"—Page 569.

Mr. Thiele tells us, in a note on the *Danske Folkesagn,* that there are still families who believe themselves to be descended from such marriages. A similar belief exists in Kerry respecting the O'Flaherty and the O'Sullivan families; and the Macnamaras, a Clare family, have their name from a tradition of the same nature. Morgan, according to Ussher, signified in the ancient British "*Born of the Sea.*" It was the real name of the celebrated Pelagius; and is at present a very common one in Wales.

Vade, the father of the famous smith Velent, was the son of king Vilkinus and a Mermaid whom he met in a wood on the sea shore in Russia.

Vilkina Saga, c. 18.

The stories of Peleus and Thetis in classical, and of king Beder and the fair Gulnare in oriental literature, may be referred to, as well as the ballad of *Rosmer Havmand* translated by Mr. Jamieson from the Kœmpe Viser, and many others.

"Paracelsus," says old Burton, "hath several stories of them" (Water devils), "how they have lived, and been married to mortal men, and so continued for several years with them, and after, upon some dislike, have forsaken them."—*Anatomie of Melancholy, p.* 47.

The Irish word Merrow, correctly written *Moruadh*, or *Morúach*, answers exactly to the English mermaid, and is the compound of *muir*, the sea, and *oigh*, a maid. It is also used to express a sea monster, like the Armoric and Cornish *morhuch*, to which it evidently bears analogy. A mermaid is called in Basse Bretagne, *Mary Morgan*. Is Mary, Marie, or is it derived from the sea? Morgan has been already mentioned.

In Irish, *Murdhucha'n*, *Muir-gheilt*, *Samhghubha*, and *Suire*, are various names for sea-nymphs or mermaids. The romantic historians of Ireland describe the *Suire*, or sea-nymphs, as playing round the ships of the Milesians when on their passage to that Island.

The poem of *Moira Borb* (to be found in Miss Brooke's Relics of Irish Poetry) celebrates the valour of the Finian heroes in the cause of a lady, who introduces herself in pretty nearly the words of the Merrow, in the foregoing story. "As mé inġean riġ fo ṫuinn." *I am the daughter of the king under the waves.*

The *cohuleen driuth* bears some resemblance to the feather dresses of the ladies, in the oriental tales of Jahanshah, and Hassan of Bassora. There is something also of the same nature in a modern German Tale. It may be explained as an enchanted cap, from *cuthdarùn*, a sort of montera or monmouth cap; and *drùadh*, a charmer or magician.

In the tale, a rock on the shore is said to look as bold as ever Kerry witness did. A Kerry witness (no offence to MacGillicuddy) signifies a witness who will swear any thing.

"The dudeen," or the pipe, "the woman," and such expressions, are examples of the practice so common among the Irish of using the article instead of the possessive pronoun. In this, and the preceding volume, there are many instances. It agrees extremely with the Greek idiom; and the late bishop of Calcutta might have found in it a strong exemplification of some points of his doctrine respecting the article. It has, at all events, a better effect than the emphatically expressed *my* of the English.

Dick calls the echo the child of his voice: the daughter, according to General Vallancey, is a literal translation of the Irish compound name for Echo, and a convincing argument of our eastern origin. "What people in the world," says that fanciful antiquary, "the orientalists and the Irish excepted, called the copy of a book the son of a book, and echo the daughter of a voice?" The General here evidently alludes to the Rabbinical mode of divination by בַּת־קוֹל, i. e. *the daughter of the voice*.

Mucalla is the Hibernian term for the "Jocosa Montis imago" of Horace, and is explained by Dr.

O'Brien, in his Irish Dictionary, as *the pig of the rock or cliff;* query, if it be not *Macalla, son of the cliff,* which General Vallancey, with his usual ingenuity in the confounding of words, has translated daughter? *Allabhair,* another Irish name for echo, or rather a compound echo, is, literally, *the cliffs game at goal,* or the bounding and rebounding of the voice, as the ball in that game.

In Iceland they assign a supernatural origin to Echo, and call it *Dvergmal* or the voice of the Dvergs or Dwarfs.

Smerwick harbour, where the scene of the tale is laid, is situated on the north side of a little "tongue" of land, which the county Kerry shoots forth into the Atlantic, and which, to use the words of Camden, is "beaten on with barking billows on both sides." It is memorable in history, from the landing of some Spaniards and Italians, in 1579, under the pope's consecrated banner, who threw up a defence there, called Fort del Ore. Sir Walter Raleigh's butchery of the garrison in cold blood still remains a subject of execration in the mouths of the Irish peasantry, and a stain upon English history, which even the pens of Spenser and Camden fail in vindicating. To it, however, we are said to be indebted for the poet's truly valuable work, "a View of the State of Ireland," undertaken for the purpose of excusing his patron, lord Grey de Wilton, then lord deputy of Ireland.

A map of Smerwick harbour, illustrative of this

event, is preserved in the State Paper Office, which that zealous and distinguished antiquary, Mr. Lemon, conjectures, from the writing, to be the performance of the author of the " Fairie Queen."

Gollerus is a small village on the eastern side of the harbour, about a quarter of a mile from the shore, near which there is a very ancient stone cell or chapel, a building probably coeval with the round tower.

FLORY CANTILLON'S FUNERAL.

The ancient burial-place of the Cantillon family was on an island in Ballyheigh Bay. This island was situated at no great distance from the shore, and at a remote period was overflowed in one of the incroachments which the Atlantic has made on that part of the coast of Kerry. The fishermen declare they have often seen the ruined walls of an old chapel beneath them in the water, as they sailed over the clear green sea, of a sunny afternoon. However this may be, it is well known that the Cantillons were, like most other Irish families, strongly attached to their ancient burial-place; and this attachment led to the custom, when any of the family died, of carrying the corpse to the sea side, where the coffin was left on the shore within reach of the tide. In the morning it had disappeared, being, as was traditionally believed, conveyed away by the ancestors of the deceased to their family tomb.

Connor Crowe, a county Clare man, was related to the Cantillons by marriage. "Connor Mac in Cruagh, of the seven quarters of Breintragh," as he was commonly called, and a proud man he was of the name. Connor, be it known, would drink a quart of salt water, for its medicinal virtues, before breakfast; and for the same reason, I suppose, double that quantity of raw whiskey between breakfast and night, which last he did with as little inconvenience to himself as any man in the barony of Moyferta; and were I to add Clanderalaw and Ibrickan, I don't think I should say wrong.

On the death of Florence Cantillon, Connor Crowe was determined to satisfy himself about the truth of this story of the old church under the sea: so when he heard the news of the old fellow's death, away with him to Ardfert, where Flory was laid out in high style, and a beautiful corpse he made.

Flory had been as jolly and as rollocking a boy in his day as ever was stretched, and his wake was in every respect worthy of him. There was all kind of entertainment and all sort of diversion at it, and no less than three girls got husbands there—more luck to them. Every thing was as it should be: all that side of the country, from Dingle to Tarbert, was at the funeral. The Keen was sung long and bitterly; and according to the family custom, the coffin was carried to Bally-heigh strand, where it was laid upon the shore with a prayer for the repose of the dead.

The mourners departed, one group after another, and at last Connor Crowe was left alone; he then pulled out his whiskey bottle, his drop of comfort as he called it, which he required, being in grief; and down he sat upon a big stone that was sheltered by a projecting rock, and partly concealed from view, to await with patience the appearance of the ghostly undertakers.

The evening came on mild and beautiful; he whistled an old air which he had heard in his childhood, hoping to keep idle fears out of his head; but the wild strain of that melody brought a thousand recollections with it, which only made the twilight appear more pensive.

"If 'twas near the gloomy tower of Dunmore, in my own sweet county, I was," said Connor Crowe, with a sigh, "one might well believe that the prisoners, who were murdered long ago, there in the vaults under the castle, would be the hands to carry off the coffin out of envy, for never a one of them was buried decently, nor had as much as a coffin amongst them all. 'Tis often, sure enough, I have heard lamentations and great mourning coming from the vaults of Dunmore Castle; but," continued he, after fondly pressing his lips to the mouth of his companion, and silent comforter, the whiskey bottle, "didn't I know all the time well enough, 'twas the dismal sounding waves working through the cliffs and hollows of the rocks, and fretting themselves to foam. Oh then, Dunmore Castle, it is you that are the gloomy looking tower on a gloomy day, with the gloomy hills behind you; when one has gloomy thoughts on their heart, and sees you like a ghost rising out of the smoke made by the kelp burners on the strand, there is, the Lord save us! as fearful a look about you as about the Blue Man's Lake at midnight. Well then, any how," said Connor, after a pause, "is it not a blessed night, though surely the moon looks mighty pale in the face? St. Senan himself between us and all kinds of harm."

It was, in truth, a lovely moonlight night; nothing was to be seen around but the dark rocks, and the white pebbly beach, upon which the sea broke with a hoarse and melancholy murmur. Connor, notwithstanding his frequent draughts, felt rather queerish, and almost began to repent his curiosity. It was certainly a solemn sight to behold the black coffin resting upon the white strand. His imagination gradually converted the deep moaning of old ocean into a mournful wail for the dead, and from the shadowy recesses of the rocks he imaged forth strange and visionary forms.

As the night advanced, Connor became weary with watching; he caught himself more than once in the fact of nodding, when suddenly giving his head a shake, he would look towards the black coffin. But the narrow house of death remained unmoved before him.

It was long past midnight, and the moon was sinking into the sea, when he heard the sound of many voices, which gradually became stronger, above the heavy and monotonous roll of the sea: he listened, and presently could distinduish a Keen, of exquisite sweetness, the notes of which rose and fell with the heaving of the waves, whose deep murmur mingled with and supported the strain!

The Keen grew louder and louder, and seemed to approach the beach, and then fell into a low plaintive wail. As it ended, Connor beheld a number of strange, and in the dim light, mysterious-looking figures, emerge from the sea, and surround the coffin, which they prepared to launch into the water.

"This comes of marrying with the creatures of earth," said one of the figures, in a clear, yet hollow tone.

"True," replied another, with a voice still

more fearful, " our king would never have commanded his gnawing white-toothed waves to devour the rocky roots of the island cemetery, had not his daughter, Durfulla, been buried there by her mortal husband!"

" But the time will come," said a third, bending over the coffin,

" When mortal eye—our work shall spy,
And mortal ear—our dirge shall hear."

" Then," said a fourth, " our burial of the Cantillons is at an end for ever!"

As this was spoken, the coffin was borne from the beach by a retiring wave, and the company of sea people prepared to follow it; but at the moment, one chanced to discover Connor Crowe, as fixed with wonder and as motionless with fear as the stone on which he sat.

" The time is come," cried the unearthly being, " the time is come; a human eye looks on the forms of ocean, a human ear has heard their voices: farewell to the Cantillons; the sons of the sea are no longer doomed to bury the dust of the earth!"

One after the other turned slowly round, and regarded Connor Crowe, who still remained as if bound by a spell. Again arose their funeral song; and on the next wave they followed the coffin. The sound of the lamentation died away, and at length nothing was heard but the rush of waters. The coffin and the train of sea people sank over the old church-yard, and never, since the funeral of old Flory Cantillon, have any of the family been carried to the strand of Ballyheigh, for conveyance to their rightful burial-place, beneath the waves of the Atlantic.

Another version of this wild and picturesque tradition has been communicated to the writer by Mr. Lynch, of the King's German legion. In both legends the locality is the same; but the name of the M'Ellicot family is substituted for that of the Cantillons. The latter, however, accords with the statement of Doctor Smith, in his History of Kerry, p. 210.

" The neighbouring inhabitants," says that writer, speaking of Ballyheigh, " show some rocks visible in this bay only at low tides, which they say are the remains of an island that was formerly the burial-place of the family of Cantillon, the ancient proprietors of Ballyheigh."

In the preceding note mention has been made of the conjugal union contracted between the human race and the inhabitants of the deep. An attachment, however, between the finny tribes and man has some foundation in fact, if we are to credit the testimony of the ancients. In the following story given by Athenæus, though dolphins do not exactly act as undertakers, they seem to have performed the part of mourners.

The dolphin, says Athenæus (Lib. 13. Cap. 8.), is of all animals the fondest of men, the most sensible, and one possessing the virtue of gratitude. Phylarchus relates, in his 12th Book, that Coiranus, the Milesian, seeing some fishermen who had caught a dolphin in their nets, and were about to cut him up, gave them some money, and prevailed on them to throw him back into the sea. Some time after happening to be shipwrecked near Myconos, all on board perished except Coiranus, who was saved by a dolphin. Coiranus died when an old man, in his own country; and the funeral happening to take place on the shore, by Miletus, a great number of dolphins appeared in the harbour on that day, and swam at a little distance along the shore after those who attended the funeral, joining, as it were, the procession, as mourners, and attending on the funeral of the man.

Pliny mentions a pretty anecdote of the friendship existing between a boy and a dolphin, which seems to have been a favourite tale, as it is also related both by Ælian and Aulus Gellius.

Connor Crowe will be recognised by those acquainted with the county Clare, as a faithful sketch from nature. The Blue Man's Lake mentioned in his soliloquy is situated in the Bog of Shragh, about four miles from Kilrush. It is so named from the tradition, that a spectral figure enveloped in a bluish flame haunts its melancholy waters.

Durfulla, the name of the sea-king's daughter, who married Flory Cantillon's ancestor, signifies *leaping water.* "Gnawing white toothed waves" is the literal translation of a common Irish epithet.

THE SOUL CAGES.

JACK DOGHERTY lived on the coast of the county Clare. Jack was a fisherman, as his father and grandfather before him had been. Like them, too, he lived all alone (but for the wife), and just in the same spot. People used to wonder why the Dogherty family were so fond of that wild situation, so far away from all human kind, and in the midst of huge shattered rocks, with nothing but the wide ocean to look upon. But they had their own good reasons for it.

The place was just the only spot on that part of the coast where any body could well live; there was a neat little creek, where a boat might lie as snug as a puffin in her nest, and out from this creek a ledge of sunken rocks ran into the sea. Now when the Atlantic, according to custom, was raging with a storm, and a good westerly wind was blowing strong on the coast, many a richly laden ship went to pieces on these rocks; and then the fine bales of cotton and tobacco, and such like things, and the pipes of wine, and the puncheons of rum, and the casks of brandy, and the kegs of Hollands that used to come ashore! Dunbeg Bay was just like a little estate to the Doghertys.

Not but they were kind and humane to a distressed sailor, if ever one had the good luck to get to land; and many a time indeed did Jack put out in his little *corragh* (which, though not quite equal to honest Andrew Hennessy's canvas life-boat, would breast the billows like any gannet), to lend a hand towards bringing off the crew from a wreck. But when the ship had gone to pieces, and the crew were all lost, who would blame Jack for picking up all he could find?

"And who is the worse of it?" said he. "For as to the king, God bless him! every body knows he's rich enough already without getting what's floating in the sea."

Jack, though such a hermit, was a goodnatured jolly fellow. No other, sure, could ever have coaxed Biddy Mahony to quit her father's snug and warm house in the middle of the town of Ennis, and to go so many miles off to live among the rocks, with the seals and sea gulls for next door neighbours. But Biddy knew that Jack was the man for a woman who wished to be comfortable and happy; for, to say nothing of the fish, Jack had the supplying of half the gentlemen's houses of the country with the *Godsends* that came into the bay. And she was right in her choice; for no woman ate, drank, or slept better, or made a prouder appearance at chapel on Sundays, than Mrs. Dogherty.

Many a strange sight, it may well be supposed, did Jack see, and many a strange sound did he hear, but nothing daunted him. So far was he from being afraid of Merrows, or such beings, that the very first wish of his heart was to fairly meet with one. Jack had heard that they were mighty like Christians, and that luck had always come out of an acquaintance with them. Never, therefore, did he dimly discern the Merrows moving along the face of the waters in their robes of mist, but he made direct for them; and many a scolding did Biddy, in her own quiet way, bestow upon Jack for spending his whole day out at sea, and bringing home no fish. Little did poor Biddy know the fish Jack was after!

It was rather annoying to Jack, that, though living in a place where the Merrows were as plenty as lobsters, he never could get a right view of one. What vexed him more was that both his father and grandfather had often and often seen them; and he even remembered hearing, when a child, how his grandfather, who was the first of the family that had settled down at the creek, had been so intimate with a Merrow, that only for fear of vexing the priest, he would have had him stand for one of his children. This, however, Jack did not well know how to believe.

Fortune at length began to think that it was only right that Jack should know as much as his father and grandfather did. Accordingly, one day when he had strolled a little farther than usual along the coast to the northward, just as he turned a point, he saw something, like to nothing he had ever seen before, perched upon a rock at a little distance out to sea: it looked green in the body, as well as he could discern at that distance, and he would have sworn, only the thing was impossible, that it had a cocked hat in its hand. Jack stood for a good half hour straining his eyes and wondering at it, and all the time the thing did not stir hand or foot. At last Jack's patience was quite worn out, and he gave a loud whistle and a hail, when the Merrow (for such it was) started up, put the cocked hat on its head, and dived down, head foremost, from the rock.

Jack's curiosity was now excited, and he constantly directed his steps towards the point; still he could never get a glimpse of the sea gentleman with the cocked hat; and with thinking and thinking about the matter, he began at last to fancy he had been only dreaming. One very rough day, however, when the sea was running mountains high, Jack Dogherty determined to give a look at the Merrow's rock (for he had always chosen a fine day before), and then he saw the strange thing cutting capers upon the top of the rock, and then diving down, and then coming up, and then diving down again.

Jack had now only to choose his time (that is, a good blowing day), and he might see the man of the sea as often as he pleased. All this, however, did not satisfy him—"much will have more;" he wished now to get acquainted with the Merrow, and even in this he succeeded. One tremendous blustering day, before he got to the point, whence he had a view of the Merrow's rock, the storm came on so furiously that Jack was obliged to take shelter in one of the caves which are so numerous along the coast; and there, to his astonishment, he saw sitting before him a thing with green hair, long green teeth, a red nose, and pig's eyes. It had a fish's tail, legs with scales on them, and short arms like fins: it wore no clothes, but had the cocked hat under its arm, and seemed engaged thinking very seriously about something.

Jack, with all his courage, was a little daunted; but now or never, thought he: so up he went boldly to the cogitating fishman, took off his hat, and made his best bow.

"Your servant, sir," said Jack.

"Your servant, kindly, Jack Dogherty," answered the Merrow.

"To be sure, then, how well your honour knows my name!" said Jack.

"Is it I not know your name, Jack Dogherty? Why, man, I knew your grandfather long before he was married to Judy Regan, your grandmother! Ah, Jack, Jack, I was fond of that grandfather of yours; he was a mighty worthy man in his time: I never met his match above or below, before or since, for sucking in a shellful of brandy. I hope, my boy," said the old fellow, with a merry twinkle in his little eyes, "I hope you're his own grandson!"

"Never fear me for that," said Jack; "if my mother had only reared me on brandy, 'tis myself that would be a sucking infant to this hour!"

"Well, I like to hear you talk so manly; you and I must be better acquainted, if it were only for your grandfather's sake. But, Jack, that father of yours was not the thing; he had no head at all."

"I'm sure," said Jack, "since your honour

lives down under the water, you must be obliged to drink a power to keep any heat in you in such a cruel, damp, *could* place. Well, I've often heard of Christians drinking like fishes: and might I be so bold as to ask where you get the spirits?"

"Where do you get them, yourself, Jack?" said the Merrow, twitching his red nose between his forefinger and thumb.

"Hubbubboo," cries Jack, "now I see how it is; but I suppose, sir, your honour has got a fine dry cellar below to keep them in."

"Let me alone for the cellar," said the Merrow, with a knowing wink of his left eye.

"I'm sure," continued Jack, "it must be mighty well worth the looking at."

"You may say that, Jack," said the Merrow; "and if you meet me here, next Monday, just at this time of the day, we will have a little more talk with one another about the matter."

Jack and the Merrow parted the best friends in the world.

On Monday they met, and Jack was not a little surprised to see that the Merrow had two cocked hats with him, one under each arm.

"Might I take the liberty to ask, sir," said Jack, "why your honour has brought the two hats with you to-day? You would not, sure, be going to give me one of them, to keep for the *curosity* of the thing?"

"No, no, Jack," said he, "I don't get my hats so easily, to part with them that way; but I want you to come down and dine with me, and I brought you the hat to dive with."

"Lord bless and preserve us!" cried Jack, in amazement, "would you want me to go down to the bottom of the salt sea ocean? Sure I'd be smothered and choked up with the water, to say nothing of being drowned! And what would poor Biddy do for me, and what would she say?"

"And what matter what she says, you *pinkeen?* Who cares for Biddy's squalling? It's long before your grandfather would have talked in that way. Many's the time he stuck that same hat on his head, and dived down boldly after me; and many's the snug bit of dinner and good shellful of brandy he and I have had together below, under the water."

"Is it really, sir, and no joke?" said Jack; "why, then, sorrow from me for ever and a day after, if I'll be a bit worse man nor my grandfather was! Here goes—but play me fair now. Here's neck or nothing!" cried Jack.

"That's your grandfather all over," said the old fellow; "so come along then, and do as I do."

They both left the cave, walked into the sea, and then swam a piece until they got to the rock. The Merrow climbed to the top of it, and Jack followed him. On the far side it was as straight as the wall of a house, and the sea beneath looked so deep that Jack was almost cowed.

"Now, do you see, Jack," said the Merrow: "just put this hat on your head, and mind to keep your eyes wide open. Take hold of my tail, and follow after me, and you 'll see what you 'll see."

In he dashed, and in dashed Jack after him boldly. They went and they went, and Jack thought they 'd never stop going. Many a time did he wish himself sitting at home by the fireside with Biddy. Yet, where was the use of wishing now, when he was so many miles as he thought below the waves of the Atlantic? Still he held hard by the Merrow's tail, slippery as it was; and, at last, to Jack's great surprise, they got out of the water, and he actually found himself on dry land at the bottom of the sea. They landed just in front of a nice house that was slated very neatly with oyster shells! and the Merrow turning about to Jack, welcomed him down.

Jack could hardly speak, what with wonder, and what with being out of breath with travelling so fast through the water. He looked about him and could see no living things, barring crabs and lobsters, of which there were plenty walking leisurely about on the sand. Overhead was the sea like a sky, and the fishes like birds swimming about in it.

"Why don't you speak, man?" said the Merrow: "I dare say you had no notion that I had such a snug little concern here as this? Are you smothered, or choked, or drowned, or are you fretting after Biddy, eh?"

"Oh! not myself, indeed," said Jack, showing his teeth with a good-humoured grin:—"but who in the world would ever have thought of seeing such a thing?"

"Well, come along and let's see what they've got for us to eat?"

Jack really was hungry, and it gave him no small pleasure to perceive a fine column of smoke rising from the chimney, announcing what was going on within. Into the house he followed the Merrow, and there he saw a good kitchen, right well provided with every thing. There was a noble dresser, and plenty of pots and pans, with two young Merrows cooking. His host then led him into the room, which was furnished shabbily enough. Not a table or a chair was there in it; nothing but planks and logs of wood to sit on, and eat off. There was, however, a good fire blazing on the hearth—a comfortable sight to Jack.

"Come now, and I'll show you where I keep —you know what," said the Merrow, with a sly look; and opening a little door, he led Jack into a fine long cellar well filled with pipes, and kegs, and hogsheads, and barrels.

"What do you say to that, Jack Dogherty?—Eh!—may be a body can't live snug under the water?"

"Never the doubt of that," said Jack, with a convincing smack of his under lip, that he really thought what he said.

They went back to the room, and found dinner laid. There was no table-cloth, to be sure—but what matter? It was not always Jack had one at home. The dinner would have been no discredit to the first house of the county on a fast day. The choicest of fish, and no wonder, was there. Turbots, and soles, and lobsters, and oysters, and twenty other kinds were on the planks at once, and plenty of the best of foreign spirits. The wines, the old fellow said, were too cold for his stomach.

Jack ate and drank till he could eat no more: then taking up a shell of brandy, "Here's to your honour's good health, sir," said he; "though, begging your pardon, it's mighty odd, that as long as we 've been acquainted, I don't know your name yet."

"That 's true, Jack," replied he; "I never thought of it before, but better late than never. My name 's Coomara."

"And a mighty decent name it is," cried Jack, taking another shellful: "here 's to your good health, Coomara, and may you live these fifty years to come!"

"Fifty years!" repeated Coomara; "I 'm obliged to you, indeed! If you had said five hundred, it would have been something worth the wishing."

"By the laws, sir," cries Jack, "*youz* live to a powerful great age here under the water! You knew my grandfather, and he 's dead and gone better than these sixty years. I 'm sure it must be a mighty healthy place to live in."

"No doubt of it; but come, Jack, keep the liquor stirring." Shell after shell did they empty, and to Jack's exceeding surprise, he found the drink never got into his head, owing, I suppose, to the sea being over them, which kept their noddles cool.

Old Coomara got exceedingly comfortable, and sung several songs; but Jack, if his life had depended on it, never could remember more than

Rum fum boodle boo,
Ripple dipple nitty dob;
Dum doo doodle coo,
Raffle taffle chittibob!

It was the chorus to one of them; and to say the truth, nobody that I know has ever been able to pick any particular meaning out of it; but that, to be sure, is the case with many a song now-a-days.

At length said he to Jack, "Now, my dear boy, if you follow me, I 'll show you my *curosities!*" He opened a little door and led Jack into a large room, where Jack saw a great many odds and ends that Coomara had picked up at one time or another. What chiefly took his attention, however, were things like lobster pots ranged on the ground along the wall.

"Well, Jack, how do you like my *curosities*?" said old Coo.

"Upon my *sowkins,* sir," said Jack, "they 're mighty well worth the looking at; but might I make so bold as to ask what these things like lobster pots are?"

"Oh! the Soul Cages, is it?"

"The what? Sir!"

"These things here that I keep the Souls in."

"*Arrah!* what Souls, sir?" said Jack in amazement: "sure the fish have got no souls in them?"

"Oh! no," replied Coo, quite coolly, "that they have not; but these are the souls of drowned sailors."

"The Lord preserve us from all harm!" muttered Jack, "how in the world did you get them?"

"Easily enough: I've only when I see a good storm coming on, to set a couple of dozen of these, and then, when the sailors are drowned and the souls get out of them under the water, the poor things are almost perished to death, not being used to the cold; so they make into my pots for shelter, and then I have them snug, and fetch them home, and keep them here dry and warm; and is it not well for them poor souls to get into such good quarters?"

Jack was so thunderstruck, he did not know what to say, so he said nothing. They went back into the dining-room and had a little more brandy, which was excellent, and then as Jack knew that it must be getting late, and as Biddy might be uneasy, he stood up, and said he thought it was time for him to be on the road.

"Just as you like, Jack," said Coo, "but take

a *duc an durrus* before you go; you 've a cold journey before you."

Jack knew better manners than to refuse the parting glass. "I wonder," said he, "will I be able to make out my way home?"

"What should ail you," said Coo, "when I 'll show you the way?

Out they went before the house, and Coomara took one of the cocked hats, and put it upon Jack's head the wrong way, and then lifted him up on his shoulder that he might launch him up into the water.

"Now," says he, giving him a heave, "you 'll come up just in the same spot you came down in, and, Jack, mind and throw me back the hat."

He canted Jack off his shoulder, and up he shot like a bubble—whirr, whirr, whiz—away he went up through the water, till he came to the very rock he had jumped off, where he found a landing-place, and then in he threw the hat, which sunk like a stone.

The sun was just going down in the beautiful sky of a calm summer's evening. *Feascor* was seen dimly twinkling in the cloudless heaven, a solitary star, and the waves of the Atlantic flashed in a golden flood of light. So Jack, perceiving it was late, set off home; but when he got there, not a word did he say to Biddy of where he had spent his day.

The state of the poor Souls cooped up in the lobster pots gave Jack a great deal of trouble, and how to release them cost him a great deal of thought. He at first had a mind to speak to the priest about the matter. But what could the priest do, and what did Coo care for the priest? Besides, Coo was a good sort of an old fellow, and did not think he was doing any harm. Jack had a regard for him too, and it also might not be much to his own credit if it were known that he used to go dine with Merrows. On the whole, he thought his best plan would be to ask Coo to dinner, and to make him drunk, if he was able, and then to take the hat and go down and turn up the pots. It was first of all necessary, however, to get Biddy out of the way; for Jack was prudent enough, as she was a woman, to wish to keep the thing secret from her.

Accordingly, Jack grew mighty pious all of a sudden, and said to Biddy, that he thought it would be for the good of both of their souls if she was to go and take her rounds at Saint John's Well, near Ennis. Biddy thought so too, and accordingly off she set one fine morning at day dawn, giving Jack a strict charge to have an eye to the place.

The coast being clear, away went Jack to the rock to give the appointed signal to Coomara, which was throwing a big stone into the water. Jack threw, and up sprang Coo!

"Good morrow, Jack," said he; "what do you want with me?"

"Just nothing at all to speak about, sir," returned Jack, "only to come and take a bit of dinner with me, if I might make so free as to ask you, and sure I 'm now after doing so."

"It 's quite agreeable, Jack, I assure you; what 's your hour?"

"Any time that 's most convenient to you, sir—say one o'clock, that you may go home, if you wish, with the day-light."

"I 'll be with you," said Coo, "never fear me."

Jack went home, and dressed a noble fish dinner, and got out plenty of his best foreign spirits, enough for that matter to make twenty men drunk. Just to the minute came Coo, with his cocked hat under his arm. Dinner was ready—they sat down, and ate and drank away manfully. Jack thinking of the poor Souls below in the pots, plied old Coo well with brandy and encouraged him to sing, hoping to put him under the table, but poor Jack forgot that he had not the sea over his own head to keep it cool. The brandy got into it and did his business for him, and Coo reeled off home, leaving his entertainer as dumb as a haddock on a Good Friday.

Jack never woke till the next morning, and then he was in a sad way. " 'Tis to no use for me thinking to make that old Rapparee drunk," said Jack, " and how in this world can I help the poor Souls out of the lobster pots?" After ruminating nearly the whole day, a thought struck him. " I have it," says he, slapping his knee; " I 'll be sworn that Coo never saw a drop of *poteen* as old as he is, and that 's the *thing* to settle him! Oh! then is not it well that Biddy will not be home these two days yet; I can have another twist at him."

Jack asked Coo again, and Coo laughed at him for having no better head, telling him, he 'd never come up to his grandfather.

" Well, but try me again," said Jack, " and I 'll be bail to drink you drunk and sober, and drunk again."

" Any thing in my power," said Coo, " to oblige you."

At this dinner, Jack took care to have his own liquor well watered, and to give the strongest brandy he had to Coo. At last, says he; " Pray, sir, did you ever drink any poteen?—any real Mountain dew?"

"No," says Coo; "what 's that, and where does it come from?"

"Oh, that 's a secret," said Jack, "but it's the right stuff—never believe me again, if 'tis not fifty times as good as brandy or rum either. Biddy's brother just sent me a present of a little drop, in exchange for some brandy, and as you 're an old friend of the family, I kept it to treat you with."

"Well, let 's see what sort of thing it is," said Coomara.

The *poteen* was the right sort. It was first rate, and had the real smack upon it. Coo was delighted; he drank and he sung, *Rum bum boodle boo* over and over again; and he laughed and he danced till he fell on the floor fast asleep. Then Jack, who had taken good care to keep himself sober, snapt up the cocked hat—ran off to the rock—leaped in, and soon arrived at Coo's habitation.

All was as still as a church-yard at midnight—not a Merrow old or young was there. In he went and turned up the pots, but nothing did he see, only he heard a sort of a little whistle or chirp as he raised each of them. At this he was surprised, till he recollected what the priest had often said, that nobody living could see the soul, no more than they could see the wind or the air! Having now done all that he could do for them, he set the pots as they were before, and sent a blessing after the poor souls, to speed them on their journey wherever they were going. Jack now began to think of returning; he put the hat on, as was right, the wrong way; but when he got out, he found the water so high over his head, that he had no hopes of ever getting up into it, now that he had not old Coomara to give him a lift. He walked about looking for a ladder, but not one could he find, and not a rock was there in sight. At last he saw a spot where the sea hung rather lower than any where else, so he resolved to try there. Just as he came to it, a big cod happened to put down his tail. Jack made a jump and caught hold of it, and the cod, all in amazement, gave a bounce and pulled Jack up. The minute the hat touched the water, pop away Jack was whisked, and up he shot like a cork, dragging the poor cod, that he forgot to let go, up with him, tail foremost. He got to the rock in no time, and without a moment's delay hurried home, rejoicing in the good deed he had done. But, meanwhile, there was fine work at home; for our friend Jack had hardly left the house on his soul-freeing expedition, when back came Biddy from her soul-saving one to the well.

When she entered the house and saw the things lying *thrie-na helah* on the table before her,

"Here's a pretty job!" said she—"that blackguard of mine—what ill-luck I had ever to marry him! He has picked up some vagabond or other, while I was praying for the good of his soul, and they've been drinking all the *poteen* that my own brother gave him, and all the spirits, to be sure, that he was to have sold to his honour."—Then hearing an outlandish kind of grunt, she looked down, and saw Coomara lying under the table.—"The blessed Virgin help me," shouted she, "if he has not made a real beast of himself! Well, well, I've often heard of a man making a beast of himself with drink!—Oh hone—oh hone—Jack, honey, what will I do with you, or what will I do without you? How can any decent woman ever think of living with a beast?"—

With such like lamentations Biddy rushed out of the house, and was going, she knew not where, when she heard the well-known voice of Jack singing a merry tune. Glad enough was Biddy to find him safe and sound, and not turned into a thing that was like neither fish nor flesh. Jack was obliged to tell her all, and Biddy, though she had half a mind to be angry with him for not telling her before, owned that he had done a great service to the poor souls. Back they both went most lovingly to the house, and Jack wakened up Coomara; and perceiving the old fellow to be rather dull, he bid him not be cast down, for 'twas many a good man's case; said it all came of his not being used to the *poteen*, and recommended him, by way of cure, to swallow a hair of the dog that bit him. Coo, however, seemed to think he had had quite enough: he got up, quite out of sorts, and without having the manners to say one word in the way of civility, he sneaked off to cool himself by a jaunt through the salt water.

Coomara never missed the souls. He and Jack continued the best friends in the world, and no one, perhaps, ever equalled Jack at freeing souls from purgatory; for he contrived fifty excuses for getting into the house below the sea, unknown to the old fellow, and then turning up the pots and letting out the souls. It vexed him, to be sure, that he could never see them; but as he knew the thing to be impossible, he was obliged to be satisfied.

Their intercourse continued for several years. However, one morning, on Jack's throwing in a stone as usual, he got no answer. He flung another, and another; still there was no reply. He went away, and returned the following morning, but it was to no purpose. As he was without the hat, he could not go down to see what had become of old Coo, but his belief was, that the old man, or the old fish, or whatever he was, had either died, or had removed away from that part of the country.

In Grimm's *Deutche Sagan*, there is a story which has a striking resemblance to the foregoing; and it is accurately translated for the sake of comparison.

A waterman once lived on good terms with a peasant, who dwelt not far from his lake; he often visited him, and at last begged that the peasant would, in return, visit him in his house under the water. The peasant consented, and went with him. There was every thing below, in the water, as in a stately palace on the land,—halls, chambers, and cabinets, with costly furniture of every description. The waterman led his guest through the whole, and showed him every thing that was in it. They came at length to a little chamber, where there were standing several new pots turned upside down. The peasant asked what was in them. "They contain," said he, "the souls of drowned people which I put under the pots, and keep them close so that they cannot get away." The peasant said nothing, and came up again on the land. The affair of the souls caused him much uneasiness for a long time, and he watched till the waterman should be gone out. When this happened, the peasant who had marked the right road down, descended into the water-house, and succeeded in finding again the little chamber; and when he was there, he turned up all the pots, one after another; immediately the souls of the drowned men ascended out of the water, and were again at liberty.

Grimm says that he was told the waterman is like any other man, only that when he opens his mouth, his green teeth may be seen; he also wears a green hat, and appears to the girls, as they go by the lake he dwells in, measures out ribbon and flings it to them.

Dunbeg Bay is situated on the coast of the county Clare, and may be readily found on any map of Ireland. Corragh, or currugh, is a small boat used by the fishermen of that part, and is formed of cow hides, or pitched cloth, strained on a frame of wickerwork. The boldness and confidence of the navigators of these fragile vessels often surprises the stranger. By the Irish poets they are invariably termed broad-chested or strong-bowed corraghs; "*Curraghaune aulin cleavorshin,*" as it is pronounced. It is the *carabus* of the later Latin writers, thus described by Isidore; Carabus, parva scapha ex vimine facta, quæ contexta crudo corio genus navigii præbet."—Isidorus, Orig. l. xviii. c. 1. It is also described in some pleasing verses by Festus Avienus. Græcè κάραβος, see Suidas and Et. Mag.

Of honest Andrew Hennessy's canvas life-boat it is only necessary to state, that the inventor, with a crew of five seamen, weathered the equinoctial gale of October 1825 (the severest remembered for many years), in an experimental passage from Cork to Liverpool. After so convincing a trial, it is to be regretted that Mr. Hennessy and his plans for the preservation of human life have not experienced more attention.

St. John's Well, whither Mrs. Dogherty journeyed to take her rounds, lies at the foot of a hill, about three miles from Ennis, and close to it is a rude altar, at which the superstitious offer up their prayers. The water of this, like other holy wells, is believed to possess the power of restoring the use of the limbs, curing defective vision, &c. Near the well there is a small lough, said to be the abode of a strange kind of fish or mermaid, which used to appear very frequently. This lady of the lake was observed resorting to the cellar of Newhall, the seat of Mr. M'Donall. The butler, perceiving the wine decrease rapidly, determined, with some of his fellow-servants, to watch for the thief, and at last they caught the mermaid in the fact of drinking it. The enraged butler threw her into a chaldron of boiling water, when she vanished, after uttering three piercing shrieks, leaving only a mass of jelly behind. Since that period, her appearances have been restricted to once in every seven years.

Merrows are said to be as fond of wine as snakes are of milk, and for the sake of it to steal on board of ships in the night time. Pausanias tells us, that the citizens of Tanagra were greatly annoyed by a Triton who frequented the neighbouring coast. By the advice of the oracle, they set a large vessel of wine on the beach, which the Triton emptied on his next visit; the liquor made him drunk, and the citizens cut off his head as he slept.

Coòmara or *cú-mara,* means the sea-hound. The Irish family of Macnamara or Maconmara are, according to tradition, descended from *cúmara,* and hence their name from *mac* a son, *con* the genitive of *cu* a greyhound, and *mara* of the sea.

The Macnamara clan inhabited the western district of the county Clare, and were dependant on the O'Briens.

Cumara's song, if indeed it be not altogether the invention of the narrator, may be considered as an extremely curious lyrical fragment. But few will feel inclined to acknowledge its genuineness, as nothing appears to be more easy than to fabricate a short effusion of this kind, or even an entire language. Psalmanazar's Formosan language is well known. Rabelais abounds in specimens. Shakespeare, in "All 's well that ends well," has tried his hand at it. Swift has given some morsels of Liliputian, Brobdignagian, and other tongues; and any one curious about fairy language has only to look into Giraldus Cambrensis. Even the inhabitants of the lower regions have had a dialect invented for them, as the following valuable extract from the Macaronica of the profound Merlinus Cocaius will prove. See the opening of the XXIV. book:

"Cra cra tif trafnot sgneflet canatanta riogna
Ecce venit gridando Charon—"

which, in a marginal note, he kindly informs us—"nec Græcum nec Hebræum, sed diabolicum est." And perhaps even the well known line of Dante, of which it is an imitation—

"Pape Satan, pape Satan Aleppè,"

is nec Latinum, nec Hebræum, sed diabolicum, also.

A translation of old Cu's song, however, it is expected, would add little to our stock of knowledge, as, judging from the indubitable specimens which exist, the remarks of the sea folk are not very profound, although they evince singular powers of observation.

Waldron, in his account of the Isle of Man, relates that an amphibious damsel was once caught, and after remaining three days on shore was allowed to escape. On plunging into the water she was welcomed by a number of her own species, who were heard to inquire what she had seen among the natives of earth. —"Nothing," she answered, "wonderful, except that they were silly enough to throw away the water in which they had boiled their eggs!"

Bochart tells us, on the authority of Alkazuinius, an Arabic author, that there is a sea-animal which exactly resembles a man, only that he has a tail; he has, moreover, a grey beard; hence he is called the old man of the sea. Once upon a time one of them was brought to a certain king, who, out of curiosity, gave him a wife. They had a son who could speak the languages of both his parents. The boy was asked one day what his father said; but as the reply must necessarily lose by translation, it is given in the original Greek. He answered, "Τὸν πάτερα λίαν θαυμάζειν ὅτι τὰ ἄλλα ζώα ἔχοιεν τοὺς κέρκυς ἐις τὸ ὄπισθεν ἄυτο̃ι δέ ἐις τὸ ἔμπροσθεν."

On the Irishisms used in the Legend of "the Soul Cages" a few words. *Arrah* is a common exclamation of surprise. It is correctly written *ara*, and, according to Dr. O'Brien, signifies a conference. A popular phrase is, "Arrah come here now," *i. e.* come here and let us talk over the matter.

Duc an Durras, Anglicè, the stirrup cup, means literally, the drink at the door; from *Deoch*, to drink, and *Doras* or *Duras*, a door. In Devonshire and Cornwall it is called *Dash and Darras*, probably a corruption of the old Cornish expression.

Rapparee was the name given to certain freebooters in the times of James and William. It is used in the story rather as a term of regard, as we sometimes employ the word rogue.

Thrie-na-helah may be translated by the English word topsy-turvey.

Pinkeen and *Sowkin* are diminutives; the former of Penk or Pink, the name of the little fish more commonly called in England, Minnow. *Sowkin* is evidently a contraction of *Soulkin*, the diminutive of soul. It answers to the German *Seelchen*, and is an old English expression, no longer, it is believed, to be met with in that country, but very common as a minor oath in Ireland.

By the Laws, is, as is well known, a softening down of a very solemn asseveration. If taken literally, people may fancy it an oath not very binding in the mouth of an Irishman, who is seldom distinguished by his profound veneration for the Statute Book. This, however, only proves that law and justice in Ireland were essentially different things; for sir John Davies, himself a lawyer, remarked, long since, how fond the natives were of justice; and it is to be hoped that a regular and impartial administration will speedily impress them as synonimes on the minds of the Irish peasantry.

Few need to be informed that the lower orders in Ireland, although their tone is different, speak the English language more grammatically than those of the same rank in England. The word *yez* or *youz* affords an instance of their attention to etymology; for as they employ *you* in speaking to a single person, they naturally enough imagined that it should be employed in the plural when addressed to more than one.

"A hair of the dog that bit him," is the common recommendation of an old toper to a young one, on the morning after a debauch.

"Shall we pluck a hair of the same wolf to-day, Proctor John?"—*Ben Jonson's Bartholomew Fair*, Act 1. Scene 1.

THE LORD OF DUNKERRON.

The lord of Dunkerron—O'Sullivan More,
Why seeks he at midnight the sea-beaten shore?
His bark lies in haven, his hounds are asleep;
No foes are abroad on the land or the deep.

Yet nightly the lord of Dunkerron is known
On the wild shore to watch and to wander alone;
For a beautiful spirit of ocean, 'tis said,
The lord of Dunkerron would win to his bed.

When, by moonlight, the waters were hush'd to
repose,
That beautiful spirit of ocean arose;
Her hair, full of lustre, just floated and fell
O'er her bosom, that heaved with a billowy swell.

Long, long had he loved her—long vainly essay'd
To lure from her dwelling the coy ocean maid;
And long had he wander'd and watch'd by the tide,
To claim the fair spirit O'Sullivan's bride!

The maiden she gazed on the creature of earth,
Whose voice in her breast to a feeling gave birth:
Then smiled; and abashed, as a maiden might be,
Looking down, gently sank to her home in the sea.

Though gentle that smile, as the moonlight above,
O'Sullivan felt 'twas the dawning of love,
And hope came on hope, spreading over his mind,
As the eddy of circles her wake left behind.

The lord of Dunkerron he plunged in the waves,
And sought, through the fierce rush of waters, their caves;
The gloom of whose depths, studded over with spars,
Had the glitter of midnight when lit up by stars.

Who can tell or can fancy the treasures that sleep
Intombed in the wonderful womb of the deep?
The pearls and the gems, as if valueless, thrown
To lie 'mid the sea-wrack concealed and unknown.

Down, down went the maid,—still the chieftain pursued;
Who flies must be followed ere she can be wooed.
Untempted by treasures, unawed by alarms,
The maiden at length he has clasp t in his arms!

They rose from the deep by a smooth-spreading
strand,
Whence beauty and verdure stretch'd over the land.
'Twas an isle of enchantment! and lightly the
breeze,
With a musical murmur, just crept through the
trees.

The haze-woven shroud of that newly born isle
Softly faded away, from a magical pile,
A palace of crystal, whose bright-beaming sheen
Had the tints of the rainbow—red, yellow, and
green.

And grottoes, fantastic in hue and in form,
Were there, as flung up—the wild sport of the
storm;
Yet all was so cloudless, so lovely, and calm,
It seemed but a region of sunshine and balm.

"Here, here shall we dwell in a dream of delight,
Where the glories of earth and of ocean unite!
Yet, loved son of earth! I must from thee away;
There are laws which e'en spirits are bound to
obey!

"Once more must I visit the chief of my race,
His sanction to gain ere I meet thy embrace.

In a moment I dive to the chambers beneath:
One cause can detain me—one only—'tis death!"

They parted in sorrow, with vows true and fond;
The language of promise had nothing beyond.
His soul all on fire, with anxiety burns:
The moment is gone—but no maiden returns.

What sounds from the deep meet his terrified ear—
What accents of rage and of grief does he hear?
What sees he? what change has come over the
    flood—
What tinges its green with a jetty of blood?

Can he doubt what the gush of warm blood would
    explain?
That she sought the consent of her monarch in
    vain!—
For see all around him, in white foam and froth,
The waves of the ocean boil up in their wroth!

The palace of crystal has melted in air,
And the dies of the rainbow no longer are there;
The grottoes with vapour and clouds are o'ercast,
The sunshine is darkness—the vision has past!

Loud, loud was the call of his serfs for their chief;
They sought him with accents of wailing and grief:

He heard, and he struggled—a wave to the shore,
Exhausted and faint, bears O'Sullivan More!

Kenmare, 27th April, 1825.

An attempt has been made at throwing into the ballad form one of the many tales told of the O'Sullivan family to the writer, by an old boatman, with whom he was becalmed an entire night in the Kenmare river, on his return from a pilgrimage to the Skellig Rocks.

Grimm relates precisely the same legend of the Elbe maid, who, it appears, in rather an unearthly fashion, used to come to the market at Magdeburg to buy meat. A young butcher fell in love with her, and followed her until he found whence she came and whither she returned. At last he went down into the water with her. They told a fisherman, who assisted them and waited for them on the bank, that if a wooden trencher with an apple on it should come up through the water, all was well; if not, it was otherwise. Shortly after, a red streak shot up; a proof that the bridegroom had not pleased the kindred of the Elbe maid, and that they had put him to death. Another variation of this legend, and the one alluded to on account of its similarity, relates that the maid went down alone, and her lover remained sitting on the bank to wait her answer. She (dutiful girl) wished to get the consent of her parents to her marriage, or to communicate the affair to her brothers. However, instead of an answer, there only appeared a spot of blood upon the water, a sign that she had been put to death.

Mr. Barry St. Leger's tale of "the Nymph of the Lurley," in his clever work, "Mr. Blount's MSS.," bears a striking resemblance to another tradition related of the O'Sullivan family, and their strange intercourse with the "spirits of the vasty deep;" particularly in the circumstance of the attempt at wounding the mermaid, and the fate of the person making it.

A well known Manx legend relates that a sea maiden once carried off a beautiful youth, of whom she became enamoured, to the Isle of Man, and conjured up a mist around the island to prevent his escape; hence it has sometimes been called the Isle of Mists. Mermaid love is an extremely common fiction, and tales founded on it are abundant, although they contain little variety of incident. In the *Ballades et Chants populaires de la Provence*, lately published, there is a very pretty tale "of *La Fée aux Cheveux Verts*," who entices a fisherman to her palace beneath the sea. The amour, as is generally the case with fairy love, produces unhappy consequences.

The Annals of the Four Masters give us rather a gigantic idea of mermaids, although expressly mentioning the delicacy and beauty of their skin. According to this veritable record (which Irish historians are so fond of quoting as an authority), Pontoppidan's

Norway kraken is not without a fair companion: "A. D. 887. A mermaid of an enormous size was cast on the north-east coast of Scotland by the sea: her height was 195 feet; her hair was 18 feet; her fingers 7 feet; and her nose 7 feet: she was all over as white as a swan."

For an account of Dunkerron the reader is referred to Smith's History of Kerry, p. 88. The castle lies about a mile below the town of Kenmare, on the west side of the river. Its present remains are part of a square keep, and one side of a castellated mansion, which probably adjoined the keep, and was built at a more recent period. The Rev. Mr. Godfrey kindly pointed out to the writer two rudely sculptured stones, which had been removed from Dunkerron castle and placed in the boat-house at Lansdown lodge. One of these bears the following inscription:

I. H. S. MARIA
DEO GRATIAS
* THIS WORK
WAS MADE THE
XX OF APRIEL
1596: BY OWEN
OSULIVAN MORE
* * * DONOGH
MAC CARTY RIEOGH.

The other, the O'Sullivan arms, in which a barbarous attempt to express the figure of a mermaid is evident above the "Manus Sullivanis."

In allusion to the galley which appears on the shield,

it may be mentioned that a favourite name of the O'Sullivans is Morty or Murty (correctly written *Muircheartach* or *Muircheardach*), which literally means "expert at sea," or an able navigator. Murrough, a common Christian name of the O'Briens, signifies "the sea hound." Murphy, Murley, &c. have doubtless a marine origin.

THE WONDERFUL TUNE.

MAURICE CONNOR was the king, and that 's no small word, of all the pipers in Munster. He could play jig and planxty without end, and Ollistrum's March, and the Eagle's Whistle, and the Hen's Concert, and odd tunes of every sort and kind. But he knew one, far more surprising than the rest, which had in it the power to set every thing dead or alive dancing.

In what way he learned it is beyond my knowledge, for he was mighty cautious about telling how he came by so wonderful a tune. At the very first note of that tune, the brogues began shaking upon the feet of all who heard it—old or young, it mattered not—just as if their brogues had the ague; then the feet began going—going—going from under them, and at last up and away with them, dancing like mad!—whisking here, there, and every where, like a straw in a storm—there was no halting while the music lasted!

Not a fair, nor a wedding, nor a patron in

the seven parishes round, was counted worth the speaking of without "blind Maurice and his pipes." His mother, poor woman, used to lead him about from one place to another, just like a dog.

Down through Iveragh—a place that ought to be proud of itself, for 'tis Daniel O'Connel's country—Maurice Connor and his mother were taking their rounds. Beyond all other places Iveragh is the place for stormy coast and steep mountains: as proper a spot it is as any in Ireland to get yourself drowned, or your neck broken on the land, should you prefer that. But, notwithstanding, in Ballinskellig bay there is a neat bit of ground, well fitted for diversion, and down from it, towards the water, is a clean smooth piece of strand—the dead image of a calm summer's sea on a moonlight night, with just the curl of the small waves upon it.

Here it was that Maurice's music had brought from all parts a great gathering of the young men and the young women—*O the darlints!*—for 'twas not every day the strand of Trafraska was stirred up by the voice of a bagpipe. The dance began; and as pretty a rinkafadda it was as ever was danced. "Brave music," said every body, "and well done," when Maurice stopped.

"More power to your elbow, Maurice, and a fair wind in the bellows," cried Paddy Dorman, a hump-backed dancing-master, who was there to keep order. "'Tis a pity," said he, "if we 'd let the piper run dry after such music; 't would be a disgrace to Iveragh, that didn't come on it since the week of the three Sundays." So, as well became him, for he was always a decent man, says he: "Did you drink, piper?"

"I will, sir," says Maurice, answering the question on the safe side, for you never yet knew piper or schoolmaster who refused his drink.

"What will you drink, Maurice?" says Paddy.

"I 'm no ways particular," says Maurice; "I drink any thing, and give God thanks, barring *raw* water: but if 'tis all the same to you, mister Dorman, may be you wouldn't lend me the loan of a glass of whiskey."

"I 've no glass, Maurice," said Paddy; "I 've only the bottle."

"Let that be no hindrance," answered Maurice; "my mouth just holds a glass to the drop; often I 've tried it, sure."

So Paddy Dorman trusted him with the bottle —more fool was he; and, to his cost, he found that though Maurice's mouth might not hold more than the glass at one time, yet, owing to the hole in his throat, it took many a filling.

"That was no bad whiskey neither," says Maurice, handing back the empty bottle.

"By the holy frost, then!" says Paddy, "'tis but *could* comfort there's in that bottle now; and 'tis your word we must take for the strength of the whiskey, for you've left us no sample to judge by:" and to be sure Maurice had not.

Now I need not tell any gentleman or lady with common understanding, that if he or she was to drink an honest bottle of whiskey at one pull, it is not at all the same thing as drinking a bottle of water; and in the whole course of my life, I never knew more than five men who could do so without being overtaken by the liquor. Of these Maurice Connor was not one, though he had a stiff head enough of his own—he was fairly tipsy. Don't think I blame him for it; 'tis often a good man's case; but true is the word that says, "when liquor's in sense is out;" and puff, at a breath, before you could say "Lord, save us!" out he blasted his wonderful tune.

'Twas really then beyond all belief or telling the dancing. Maurice himself could not keep quiet; staggering now on one leg, now on the other, and rolling about like a ship in a cross sea, trying to humour the tune. There was his mother too, moving her old bones as light as the youngest girl of them all; but her dancing, no, nor the dancing of all the rest, is not worthy the speaking about to the work that was going on down upon the strand. Every inch of it covered with all manner of fish jumping and plunging about to the music, and every moment more and more would tumble in out of the water, charmed by the wonderful tune. Crabs of monstrous size spun round and round on one claw with the nimbleness of a dancing-master, and twirled and tossed their other claws about like limbs that did not belong to them. It was a sight surprising to behold. But perhaps you may have heard of father Florence Conry, a Franciscan friar, and a great Irish poet; *bolg an dàna,* as they used to call him—a wallet of poems. If you have not, he was as pleasant a man as one would wish to drink with of a hot summer's day; and he has rhymed out all about the dancing fishes so neatly, that it would be a thousand pities not to give you his verses; so here 's my hand at an upset of them into English:

The big seals in motion,
Like waves of the ocean,
    Or gouty feet prancing,
Came heading the gay fish,
Crabs, lobsters, and cray fish,
    Determined on dancing.

The sweet sounds they follow'd,
The gasping cod swallow'd;
    'Twas wonderful, really!

And turbot and flounder,
'Mid fish that were rounder,
Just caper'd as gaily.

John-dories came tripping;
Dull hake by their skipping
To frisk it seem'd given;
Bright mackrel went springing,
Like small rainbows winging
Their flight up to heaven.

The whiting and haddock
Left salt water paddock
This dance to be put in:
Where skate with flat faces
Edged out some odd plaices;
But soles kept their footing.

Sprats and herrings in powers
Of silvery showers
All number out-number'd.
And great ling so lengthy
Were there in such plenty
The shore was encumber'd.

The scollop and oyster
Their two shells did roister,
Like castanets fitting;

While limpeds moved clearly,
And rocks very nearly
With laughter were splitting.

Never was such an ullabulloo in this world, before or since; 'twas as if heaven and earth were coming together; and all out of Maurice Connor's wonderful tune!

In the height of all these doings, what should there be dancing among the outlandish set of fishes but a beautiful young woman—as beautiful as the dawn of day! She had a cocked hat upon her head; from under it her long green hair—just the colour of the sea—fell down behind, without hinderance to her dancing. Her teeth were like rows of pearl; her lips for all the world looked like red coral; and she had an elegant gown, as white as the foam of the wave, with little rows of purple and red sea weeds settled out upon it; for you never yet saw a lady, under the water or over the water, who had not a good notion of dressing herself out.

Up she danced at last to Maurice, who was flinging his feet from under him as fast as hops—for nothing in this world could keep still while that tune of his was going on—and says she to him, chaunting it out with a voice as sweet as honey—

"I'm a lady of honour
Who live in the sea;
Come down, Maurice Connor,
And be married to me.
Silver plates and gold dishes
You shall have, and shall be
The king of the fishes,
When you're married to me."

Drink was strong in Maurice's head, and out he chaunted in return for her great civility. It is not every lady, may be, that would be after making such an offer to a blind piper; therefore 'twas only right in him to give her as good as she gave herself—so says Maurice,

"I'm obliged to you, madam:
Off a gold dish or plate,
If a king, and I had 'em,
I could dine in great state.
With your own father's daughter
I'd be sure to agree;
But to drink the salt water
Wouldn't do so with me!

The lady looked at him quite amazed, and swinging her head from side to side like a great scholar,

"Well," says she, "Maurice, if you 're not a poet, where is poetry to be found?"

In this way they kept on at it, framing high compliments; one answering the other, and their feet going with the music as fast as their tongues. All the fish kept dancing too: Maurice heard the clatter and was afraid to stop playing lest it might be displeasing to the fish, and not knowing what so many of them may take it into their heads to do to him if they got vexed.

Well, the lady with the green hair kept on coaxing of Maurice with soft speeches, till at last she overpersuaded him to promise to marry her, and be king over the fishes, great and small. Maurice was well fitted to be their king, if they wanted one that could make them dance; and he surely would drink, barring the salt water, with any fish of them all.

When Maurice's mother saw him, with that unnatural thing in the form of a green-haired lady as his guide, and he and she dancing down together so lovingly to the water's edge, through the thick of the fishes, she called out after him to stop and come back. "Oh then," says she, "as if I was not widow enough before, there he is going away from me to be married to that scaly woman. And who knows but 'tis grandmother I may be to a hake or a cod—Lord help and pity me, but 'tis a mighty unnatural thing!—and may be 'tis boiling and eating my own grandchild I'll be, with a bit of salt butter, and I not knowing it!—Oh Maurice, Maurice, if there's any love or nature left in you, come back to your own *ould* mother, who reared you like a decent christian!"

Then the poor woman began to cry and ullagoane so finely that it would do any one good to hear her.

Maurice was not long getting to the rim of the water; there he kept playing and dancing on as if nothing was the matter, and a great thundering wave coming in towards him ready to swallow him up alive; but as he could not see it, he did not fear it. His mother it was who saw it plainly through the big tears that were rolling down her cheeks; and though she saw it, and her heart was aching as much as ever mother's heart ached for a son, she kept dancing, dancing, all the time for the bare life of her. Certain it was she could not help it, for Maurice never stopped playing that wonderful tune of his.

He only turned the bothered ear to the sound of his mother's voice, fearing it might put him out in his steps, and all the answer he made back was—

"Whisht with you, mother—sure I'm going

And may be 'tis boiling and eating my own grandchild I'll be

Published Decr 1st [illegible] by J. Murray, London

to be king over the fishes down in the sea, and for a token of luck, and a sign that I 'm alive and well, I 'll send you in, every twelvemonth on this day, a piece of burned wood to Trafraska." Maurice had not the power to say a word more, for the strange lady with the green hair seeing the wave just upon them, covered him up with herself in a thing like a cloak with a big hood to it, and the wave curling over twice as high as their heads, burst upon the strand, with a rush and a roar that might be heard as far as Cape Clear.

That day twelvemonth the piece of burned wood came ashore in Trafraska. It was a queer thing for Maurice to think of sending all the way from the bottom of the sea. A gown or a pair of shoes would have been something like a present for his poor mother; but he had said it, and he kept his word. The bit of burned wood regularly came ashore on the appointed day for as good, ay, and better than a hundred years. The day is now forgotten, and may be that is the reason why people say how Maurice Connor has stopped sending the luck-token to his mother. Poor woman, she did not live to get as much as one of them; for what through the loss of Maurice, and the fear of eating her own grandchildren, she died in three weeks after the dance—some say it was the fatigue that killed her, but whichever it was, Mrs. Connor was decently buried with her own people.

Seafaring people have often heard, off the coast of Kerry, on a still night, the sound of music coming up from the water; and some, who have had good ears, could plainly distinguish Maurice Connor's voice singing these words to his pipes:—

Beautiful shore, with thy spreading strand,
Thy crystal water, and diamond sand;
Never would I have parted from thee
But for the sake of my fair ladie.

The wonderful effects of music on brutes, and even inanimate matter, have been the theme of traditions in all ages. Trees and rocks gave ear to the tones of the Orphean lyre; the stones of Thebes ranged themselves in harmony to the strains of Amphion; the dolphin, delighted by the music of Arion, bore him in safety through the seas; even

"Rude Heiskar's seal through surges dark,
Will long pursue the minstrel's bark."

Lord of the Isles, c. i. st. 2.

The tales of Germany, and other countries, contain instances of magically endowed tunes. The effect of Oberon's horn is now well known in this country through Weber's opera, and Mr. Sotheby's elegant translation of Wieland's poem.

In Hogg's ballad of the Witch of Fife, the pipe of the "Wee wee man" makes

> "—the troutis laup out of the Leven Loch
> Charmit with the melodye."

And as to "fish out of water" feeling uncomfortable, Irish fish are said occasionally to prefer dry land. For this, if the language of nature be that of truth, we have no less an authority than Mr. Joseph Cooper Walker, the historian of the Irish bards, and a distinguished writer on matters of taste.

"Mr. O'Halloran informs me," says Mr. Walker, "that there is preserved in the Leabher Lecan, or Book of Sligo, a beautiful poem on the storm that arose on the second landing of the Milesians, which is attributed to Amergin. In this poem there appears a boldness of metaphor which a cold critic would despise, because it offends against the rules of Aristotle, though the Stagyrite was not then born: *however, it is the language of Nature!* The author, in order to heighten the horrors of the storm, represents the fish as being so much terrified, that they quit their element for dry land:—

> Inseaċ Nuir, mollaċ Tir;
> Tornaidein eisc lasc do ṫuind,
> Re taiḃ na Fairrce ruad;
> Cas air Find," &c.

The odd tunes mentioned as being known to Maurice Connor are great favourites in Ireland. "The Eagle's Whistle" is a singularly wild strain, which was a march or war-tune of the O'Donoghues, and is not to be met with in print. "The Hens' Concert" has been published in O'Farrell's Companion for the Pipes, and is a melodious imitation of the *tuc-tuc-a-túc-too* of the barn-door gentry. "Ollistrum's March" may be found in Researches in the South of Ireland, p. 116.

The Rinka fada is a national dance mentioned in a note in the tale of "Master and Man," in the preceding volume. It is said to mean "the long dance," from the Irish words *Rinceadth*, a dance, and *fada*, long. In Ben Jonson's Irish Masque, the words *fading* and *faders* occur; on the former Mr. Gifford observes: "This word, which was the burthen of a popular Irish song, gave name to a dance frequently mentioned by our old dramatists. Both the song and the dance appear to have been of a licentious character, and merit no further elucidation." Notwithstanding the high critical reputation of the late editor of the Quarterly, the writer, in justice to his country, must state his ignorance of any such Irish song as that mentioned by Mr. Gifford; although, from the attention which he has paid to the subject, and his personal intercourse with the peasantry, it could hardly have escaped his acquaintance. He has frequently witnessed the Rinka fada performed, but has never observed the really graceful movements of that dance to partake of licentiousness. The mere explanation, that

Feadán is the Irish for a pipe or reed, and *Feadánach*, a piper, appears to be all the comment which the passage in "rare Ben" requires. But Mr. Gifford was fond of volunteering incorrect information respecting Ireland: witness his note on "Harper," which occurs in the Masque of the Metamorphosed Gipsies, and where a reference to Simon's work on Coins would have prevented a series of inaccuracies uncalled for by the text.

"When liquor's in, the wit is out,"—a common Irish saying; resembles the old legend still to be seen over the cellar-door of Doddershall Park, Bucks, the venerable seat of colonel Pigott, where it was put up about the time of Elizabeth:

"Welcome, my freinde, drinke with a noble hearte,
But yet, before you drinke too much, departe;
For though good drinke will make a coward stout,
Yet when too much is in the wit is out."

Father Conry's poem respecting the dancing fish is freely translated from the Irish. The concluding verse of the tale, which, it is said, Maurice Connor has been heard singing under the water, is almost a literal translation of the following rann from the song of Deardra:

Ionṁun traiġin, is tréan traiġ,
Ionṁun uisge an ġainiṁ ġlain;
Moċa dtiocfuinn aisde on oir,
Nuna dtiocfuinn re mionṁuin.

Specimens of this beautiful poem have been given by Dr. Neilson in his Irish grammar (Dublin, 1808), to which the reader is referred.

Maurice is said to have turned "the bothered ear" to his mother. This Hiberno Anglicism is exactly the same as the English phrase "turning the deaf ear;" deaf being, in the Iberno Celtic, *Bódhar*. The word bother, indeed, appears to have in some degree become naturalized in England:

"O Kitty Clover, she bothers me so, &c."

Smith, in his History of Kerry (p. 102), thus describes the scene of the dance at Trafraska:—"Near the mouth of the river Inny there is a fine extensive strand, which I mention because it is almost the only smooth place that a person might venture to put an horse to gallop for many miles round it. It is esteemed also a rarity, all the cliffs of the coast being exceeding high, and washed by the ocean at low water."

FAIRY LEGENDS.

THE DULLAHAN.

———— "Men whose heads
Do grow beneath their shoulders."
SHAKSPEARE.

"Says the friar, 'tis strange headless horses should trot."
OLD SONG.

THE DULLAHAN.

THE GOOD WOMAN.

In a pleasant and not unpicturesque valley of the White Knight's Country, at the foot of the Galtee mountains, lived Larry Dodd and his wife Nancy. They rented a cabin and a few acres of land, which they cultivated with great care, and its crops rewarded their industry. They were independent and respected by their neighbours; they loved each other in a marriageable sort of way, and few couples had altogether more the appearance of comfort about them.

Larry was a hard working, and, occasionally, a hard drinking, Dutch-built, little man, with a fiddle head and a round stern; a steady-going straight-forward fellow, barring when he carried too much whiskey, which, it must be confessed, might occasionally prevent his walking the chalked line with perfect philomathical accuracy. He had a moist ruddy countenance, rather inclined to an expression of gravity, and particularly so in the morning; but, taken all together, he was generally looked upon as a marvellously proper person, notwithstanding he had, every day in the year, a sort of unholy dew upon his face, even in the coldest weather, which gave rise to a supposition, (amongst censorious persons, of course), that Larry was apt to indulge in strong and frequent potations. However, all men of talents have their faults—indeed, who is without them—and as Larry, setting aside his domestic virtues and skill in farming, was decidedly the most distinguished breaker of horses for forty miles round, he must be in some degree excused, considering the inducements of "the stirrup cup," and the fox-hunting society in which he mixed, if he had also been the greatest drunkard in the county—but in truth this was not the case.

Larry was a man of mixed habits, as well in his mode of life and his drink, as in his costume. His dress accorded well with his character—a sort of half-and-half between farmer and horse-jockey. He wore a blue coat of coarse cloth, with short skirts, and a stand-up collar; his waistcoat was red, and his lower habiliments were made of leather, which in course of time had shrunk so much that they fitted like a second skin, and long use had absorbed their moisture to such a degree that they made a strange sort of crackling noise as he walked along. A hat covered with oil skin; a cutting-whip, all worn and jagged at the end; a pair of second-hand, or, to speak more correctly, second-footed, greasy top-boots, that seemed never to have imbibed a refreshing draught of Warren's blacking of matchless lustre!—and one spur without a rowel, completed the every-day dress of Larry Dodd.

Thus equipped was Larry returning from Cashel, mounted on a rough-coated and wall-eyed nag, though, notwithstanding these and a few other trifling blemishes, a well-built animal; having just purchased the said nag, with a fancy that he could make his own money again of his bargain, and, maybe, turn an odd penny more by it at the ensuing Kildorrery fair. Well pleased with himself, he trotted fair and easy along the road in the delicious and lingering twilight of a lovely June evening, thinking of nothing at all, only whistling, and wondering would horses always be so low. "If they go at this rate," said he to himself, "for half nothing, and that paid in butter buyer's notes, who would be the fool to walk?" This very thought, indeed, was passing in his mind, when his attention was roused by a woman pacing quickly by the side of his horse, and hurrying on, as if endeavouring to reach her destination before the night closed in. Her figure, considering the long strides she took, appeared to be under the common size—rather of the dumpy order; but further, as to whether the damsel was young or old, fair or brown, pretty or ugly, Larry could form no precise notion, from her wearing a large cloak (the usual garb of the female Irish peasant), the hood of which was turned up, and completely concealed every feature.

Enveloped in this mass of dark and concealing drapery, the strange woman, without much exertion, contrived to keep up with Larry Dodd's steed for some time, when his master very civilly offered her a lift behind him, as far as he was going her way. "Civility begets civility," they say; however, he received no answer; and thinking that the lady's silence proceeded only from bashfulness, like a man of true gallantry, not a word more said Larry, until he pulled up by the side of a gap, and then says he, "*Ma colleen beg**, just jump up behind me, without a word more, though never a one have you spoke, and I'll take you safe and sound through the lonesome bit of road that is before us."

She jumped at the offer, sure enough, and up

* My little girl.

with her on the back of the horse as light as a feather. In an instant there she was seated up behind Larry, with her hand and arm buckled round his waist holding on.

"I hope you 're comfortable there, my dear," said Larry, in his own good-humoured way; but there was no answer; and on they went—trot, trot, trot—along the road; and all was so still and so quiet that you might have heard the sound of the hoofs on the limestone a mile off: for that matter there was nothing else to hear except the moaning of a distant stream, that kept up a continued *cronane**, like a nurse *hushoing*. Larry, who had a keen ear, did not however require so profound a silence to detect the click of one of the shoes. "'Tis only loose the shoe is," said he to his companion, as they were just entering on the lonesome bit of road of which he had before spoken. Some old trees, with huge trunks, all covered, and irregular branches festooned with ivy, grew over a dark pool of water, which had been formed as a drinking-place for cattle; and in the distance was seen the majestic head of Galtee-more. Here the horse, as if in grateful recognition, made a dead halt; and Larry, not knowing what vicious tricks his new purchase might have, and unwilling

* A monotonous song; a drowsy humming noise.

that through any odd chance the young woman should get *spilt* in the water, dismounted, thinking to lead the horse quietly by the pool.

" By the piper's luck, that always found what he wanted," said Larry, recollecting himself, " I've a nail in my pocket: 'tis not the first time I've put on a shoe, and may be it wo'n't be the last; for here is no want of paving-stones to make hammers in plenty."

No sooner was Larry off than off with a spring came the young woman just at his side. Her feet touched the ground without making the least noise in life, and away she bounded like an ill-mannered wench, as she was, without saying " by your leave," or no matter what else. She seemed to glide rather than run, not along the road, but across a field, up towards the old ivy-covered walls of Kilnaslattery church—and a pretty church it was.

" Not so fast, if you please, young woman—not so fast," cried Larry, calling after her; but away she ran, and Larry followed, his leathern garment, already described, crack, crick, crackling at every step he took. " Where 's my wages?" said Larry: " *Thorum pog, ma colleen oge* *,—sure I've earned a kiss from your pair of pretty

* Give me a kiss, my young girl.

lips—and I'll have it too!" But she went on faster and faster, regardless of these and other flattering speeches from her pursuer; at last she came to the churchyard wall, and then over with her in an instant.

"Well, she's a mighty smart creature anyhow. To be sure, how neat she steps upon her pasterns! Did any one ever see the like of that before;—but I'll not be baulked by any woman that ever wore a head, or any ditch either," exclaimed Larry, as with a desperate bound he vaulted, scrambled, and tumbled over the wall into the churchyard. Up he got from the elastic sod of a newly made grave in which Tade Leary that morning was buried—rest his soul!—and on went Larry, stumbling over head-stones and foot-stones, over old graves and new graves, pieces of coffins, and the skulls and bones of dead men—the Lord save us!—that were scattered about there as plenty as paving-stones; floundering amidst great overgrown dock-leaves and brambles that, with their long prickly arms, tangled round his limbs, and held him back with a fearful grasp. Mean time the merry wench in the cloak moved through all these obstructions as evenly and as gaily as if the churchyard, crowded up as it was with graves and gravestones (for people came to be buried there from far and near), had been the floor of a dancing-room. Round and round the walls of the old church she went. "I'll just wait," said Larry, seeing this, and thinking it all nothing but a trick to frighten him; "when she comes round again, if I don't take the kiss, I won't, that's all, —and here she is!" Larry Dodd sprung forward with open arms, and clasped in them—a woman, it is true—but a woman without any lips to kiss, by reason of her having no head!

"Murder!" cried he. "Well, that accounts for her not speaking." Having uttered these words, Larry himself became dumb with fear and astonishment; his blood seemed turned to ice, and a dizziness came over him; and, staggering like a drunken man, he rolled against the broken window of the ruin, horrified at the conviction that he had actually held a Dullahan in his embrace!

When he recovered to something like a feeling of consciousness, he slowly opened his eyes, and then, indeed, a scene of wonder burst upon him. In the midst of the ruin stood an old wheel of torture, ornamented with heads, like Cork gaol, when the heads of Murty Sullivan and other gentlemen were stuck upon it. This was plainly visible in the strange light which spread itself around. It was fearful to behold, but Larry could not choose but look, for his limbs were powerless through the wonder and the fear. Useless as it was, he would have called for help, but his tongue cleaved to the roof of his mouth, and not one word could he say. In short, there was Larry gazing through a shattered window of the old church, with eyes bleared and almost starting from their sockets; his breast rested on the thickness of the wall, over which, on one side, his head and outstretched neck projected, and on the other, although one toe touched the ground, it derived no support from thence: terror, as it were, kept him balanced. Strange noises assailed his ears, until at last they tingled painfully to the sharp clatter of little bells which kept up a continued ding—ding—ding—ding: marrowless bones rattled and clanked, and the deep and solemn sound of a great bell came booming on the night wind.

'Twas a spectre rung
That bell when it swung—
Swing-swang!
And the chain it squeaked,
And the pulley creaked,
Swing-swang!

And with every roll
Of the deep death toll
Ding-dong!

The hollow vault rang
As the clapper went bang,
Ding-dong!

It was strange music to dance by; nevertheless, moving to it, round and round the wheel set with skulls, were well dressed ladies and gentlemen, and soldiers and sailors, and priests and publicans, and jockeys and jennys, but all without their heads. Some poor skeletons, whose bleached bones were ill covered by moth-eaten palls, and who were not admitted into the ring, amused themselves by bowling their brainless noddles at one another, which seemed to enjoy the sport beyond measure.

Larry did not know what to think; his brains were all in a mist, and losing the balance which he had so long maintained, he fell headforemost into the midst of the company of Dullahans.

"I'm done for and lost for ever," roared Larry, with his heels turned towards the stars, and souse down he came.

"Welcome, Larry Dodd, welcome," cried every head, bobbing up and down in the air. "A drink for Larry Dodd," shouted they, as with one voice, that quavered like a shake on the bagpipes. No sooner said than done, for a player at heads, catching his own as it was bowled at him, for fear of its going astray, jumped up, put the head, without a word, under his left arm, and, with the right stretched out, presented a brimming cup to Larry, who, to show his manners, drank it off like a man.

"'Tis capital stuff," he would have said, which surely it was, but he got no further than cap, when decapitated was he, and his head began dancing over his shoulders like those of the rest of the party. Larry, however, was not the first man who lost his head through the temptation of looking at the bottom of a brimming cup. Nothing more did he remember clearly, for it seems body and head being parted is not very favourable to thought, but a great hurry scurry with the noise of carriages and the cracking of whips.

When his senses returned, his first act was to put up his hand to where his head formerly grew, and to his great joy there he found it still. He then shook it gently, but his head remained firm enough, and somewhat assured at this, he proceeded to open his eyes and look around him. It was broad daylight, and in the old church of Kilnaslattery he found himself lying, with that head, the loss of which he had anticipated, quietly resting, poor youth, "upon the lap of earth." Could it have been an ugly dream? "Oh no," said Larry, "a dream could never have brought me here, stretched on the flat of my back, with that death's head and cross marrow bones forenenting me on the fine old tombstone there that was *faced* by Pat Kearney* of Kilcrea—but where is the horse?" He got up slowly, every joint aching with pain from the bruises he had received, and went to the pool of water, but no horse was there. "'Tis home I must go," said Larry, with a rueful countenance; "but how will I face Nancy?—what will I tell her about the horse, and the seven I. O. U.'s that he cost me?—'Tis them Dullahans that have made their own of him from me—the horsestealing robbers of the world, that have no fear of the gallows!—but what's gone is gone, that's a clear case!"—so saying, he turned his steps homewards, and arrived at his cabin about noon without encountering any further adventures. There he found Nancy, who, as he expected, looked as black as a thundercloud at him for being out all night. She listened to the marvellous relation which he gave with exclamations of astonishment, and when he had concluded, of grief, at the loss of the horse that he had paid for like an honest man in I. O. U.'s, three of which she knew to be as good as gold.

* *Faced*, so written by the Chantrey of Kilcrea for "*fecit.*"

"But what took you up to the old church at all, out of the road, and at that time of the night, Larry?" inquired his wife.

Larry looked like a criminal for whom there was no reprieve; he scratched his head for an excuse, but not one could he muster up, so he knew not what to say.

"Oh! Larry, Larry," muttered Nancy, after waiting some time for his answer, her jealous fears during the pause rising like barm; "'tis the very same way with you as with any other man—you are all alike for that matter—I've no pity for you—but, confess the truth!"

Larry shuddered at the tempest which he perceived was about to break upon his devoted head. "Nancy," said he, "I do confess:—it was a young woman without any head that ——"

His wife heard no more. "A woman I knew it was," cried she; "but a woman without a head, Larry!—well, it is long before Nancy Gollagher ever thought it would come to that with her!—that she would be left dissolute and alone here by her *baste* of a husband, for a woman without a head!—O father, father! and O mother, mother! it is well you are low to-day!—that you don't see this affliction and disgrace to your daughter that you reared decent and tender. O Larry, you villian, you 'll be the death of your lawful wife going after such O—O—O—"

"Well," says Larry, putting his hands in his coat-pockets, "least said is soonest mended. Of the young woman I know no more than I do of Moll Flanders; but this I know, that a woman without a head may well be called a Good Woman, because she has no tongue!"

How this remark operated on the matrimonial dispute history does not inform us. It is, however, reported that the lady had the last word.

Mr. O'Reilly, author of the best Irish Dictionary extant, respecting the name Dullahan thus expresses himself in a communication to the writer.

"Dulachan (in Irish Dubhlachan) signifies a dark, sullen person. The word Durrachan, or Dullahan, by which in some places the goblin is known, has the same signification. It comes from *Dorr*, or *Durr*, anger, or *Durrach*, malicious, fierce, &c." The correctness of this last etymology may be questioned, as *Dubh*, black, is evidently a component part of the word.

Headless people are not peculiar to Ireland, although there alone they seem to have a peculiar name. Legends respecting them are to be found in most coun-

"O Larry you villain you'll be the death of me going after such O . O . O ..."

tries. It cannot be asserted that the ancients had any idea of people appearing after death without heads, but they firmly believed that whole nations contrived to live without them. St. Augustine, whose veracity it is to be supposed no one will question, not merely heard of them, but actually preached the gospel to such beings. In his 37th sermon, Ad Fratres in Eremo, he thus expresses himself. "Ego jam Episcopus Hipponensis eram et cum quibusdam servis Christi ad Æthiopiam perrexi ut eis sanctum Christi Evangelium prædicarem et vidimus ibi multos homines ac mulieres *capita non habentes.*" Kornmann in his "de Miraculis Vivorum" (Frankf. 1694, p. 58) endeavours to account, philosophically, for the production of headless people.

If one saint preached to people "capita non habentes," the history of other saints will prove that the head is not so essential a part of man as is generally believed. The Legend of St. Denis, who, *sans tête,* walked from Paris to the place which now bears his name, is too well known to require repetition. At Zaragosa, in Spain, there is a church called Engracia, the patron saint of which is said to have marched a league, carrying his head in his hands, talking all the way; and in this manner he presented himself at the gate of the convent. The marvellous expertness of the Orrilo of Bojardo and Ariosto at sticking on his head and limbs, when they chanced to be struck off by the adverse knight, must be familiar to the Italian reader. His chase of Astolpho, who gallops off with the head, far exceeds the sober walk of the aforesaid patron saints. See Orlando Furioso, c. 15.

Blind Harry records the adventure of an Irish chieftain who pitched his head at the renowned Sir William Wallace, which Sir William, dexterously catching by the hair, flung back at his adversary.

The idea of decollated persons walking probably began thus:—"The old painters represented the martyrs by characteristic badges, allusive of the mode of their execution; some with a knife in the bosom; others, who were decapitated, with their heads upon a table hard by, or in their hands. Hence, perhaps, arose the singular sign, still so great a favourite with our oil-men, 'The good woman,' originally expressive of a female saint; a holy or good woman, who had met her death by the privation of her head." There is no authority to prove that headless people were unable to speak; on the contrary, a variation of the story of the Golden Mountain given in a note in the *Kindermärchen,* relates, that a servant *without a head* informed the fisherman (who was to achieve the adventure), of the enchantment of the king's daughter, and of the mode of liberating her. How by the waggery of after ages the good woman came to be converted down into the silent woman, as if it were a matter of necessity, is thus explained by the poet:

"A silent woman, sir! you said—
Pray, was she painted without head?
Yes, sir, she was!—you never read on
A silent woman with her head on:

Besides, you know, there's nought but speaking
Can keep a woman's heart from breaking!"

Mr. M. W. Praed, in his pretty tale of Lillian, by an ingenious metaphor of a beautiful idiot, would explain a headless woman.

"And hence the story had ever run,
That the fairest of dames was a headless one."

To pass from the living to the dead. "The Irish Dullahan," said a high authority on such matters, "puts me in mind of a spectre at Drumlanrick castle of no less a person than the duchess of Queensberry—'Fair Kitty, blooming, young, and gay,'—who, instead of setting fire to the world in mamma's chariot, amuses herself with wheeling her own head in a wheelbarrow through the great gallery."

At Odense, in the Island of Funen, the people relate that a priest, who seduced a girl and murdered her babe, was buried alive for his crimes. His Ghost is now condemned to walk, and Sunday children (those born on Sunday, who are gifted with the power of seeing what is invisible to other eyes) have beheld him going about with his *head under his arm.*—*Thiele's Danske Folksagn*, vol. ii. p. 84.

In notes on the subsequent stories of this section, headless appearances, connected with horses and carriages, will be noticed. Such apparitions are sometimes looked on as the forerunners of death. Camerarius, in his Operæ Subseciva, c. i. p. 336., says, It not unfrequently happens in monasteries that the spectres (wraiths) of monks and nuns, whose death is at hand, are seen in the chapel, occupying their usual seats, but *without* heads. Dr. Ferrier, in his Theory of Apparitions, speaking of second sight in Scotland, (p. 65) mentions an old northern chieftain, who owned to a relative of his (Dr. F's.) "that the door" (of the room in which they and some ladies were sitting) "had appeared to open, and that a little woman *without* a head had entered the room;—that the apparition indicated the sudden death of some person of his acquaintance," &c.

This last circumstance of death being presaged by apparitions without heads seems to have something symbolical in it, as it was very natural to denote the cessation of life by a figure devoid of the seat of sensation and thought.

HANLON'S MILL.

ONE fine summer's evening Michael Noonan went over to Jack Brien's, the shoemaker, at Ballyduff, for the pair of brogues which Jack was mending for him. It was a pretty walk the way he took, but very lonesome; all along by the riverside, down under the oak-wood, till he came to Hanlon's mill, that used to be, but that had gone to ruin many a long year ago.

Melancholy enough the walls of that same mill looked; the great old wheel, black with age, all covered over with moss and ferns, and the bushes all hanging down about it. There it stood, silent and motionless; and a sad contrast it was to its former busy clack, with the stream which once gave it use rippling idly along.

Old Hanlon was a man that had great knowledge of all sorts; there was not an herb that grew in the field but he could tell the name of it and its use, out of a big book he had written, every word of it in the real Irish *karacter*. He kept a school once, and could teach the Latin; that surely is a blessed tongue all over the wide world; and

I hear tell as how "the great Burke" went to school to him. Master Edmund lived up at the old house, there, which was then in the family, and it was the Nagles that got it afterwards, but they sold it.

But it was Michael Noonan's walk I was about speaking of. It was fairly between lights, the day was clean gone, and the moon was not yet up, when Mick was walking smartly across the Inch. Well, he heard, coming down out of the wood, such blowing of horns and hallooing, and the cry of all the hounds in the world, and he thought they were coming after him; and the galloping of the horses, and the voice of the whipper-in, and he shouting out, just like the fine old song,

"Hallo Piper, Lily, agus Finder;"

and the echo over from the gray rock across the river giving back every word as plainly as it was spoken. But nothing could Mick see, and the shouting and hallooing following him every step of the way till he got up to Jack Brien's door; and he was certain, too, he heard the clack of old Hanlon's mill going, through all the clatter. To be sure, he ran as fast as fear and his legs could carry him, and never once looked behind him, well knowing that the Duhallow hounds were out in quite another quarter that day, and that nothing good could come out of the noise of Hanlon's mill.

Well, Michael Noonan got his brogues, and well heeled they were, and well pleased was he with them; when who should be seated at Jack Brien's before him, but a gossip of his, one Darby Haynes, a mighty decent man, that had a horse and car of his own, and that used to be travelling with it, taking loads like the royal mail coach between Cork and Limerick; and when he was at home, Darby was a near neighbour of Michael Noonan's.

"Is it home you're going with the brogues this blessed night?" said Darby to him.

"Where else would it be?" replied Mick: "but, by my word, 'tis not across the Inch back again I'm going, after all I heard coming here; 'tis to no good that old Hanlon's mill is busy again."

"True, for you," said Darby; "and may be you'd take the horse and car home for me, Mick, by way of company, as 'tis along the road you go. I'm waiting here to see a sister's son of mine that I expect from Kilcoleman." "That same I'll do," answered Mick, "with a thousand welcomes." So Mick drove the car fair and easy, knowing that the poor beast had come off a long journey; and Mick—God reward him for it—

was always tender-hearted and good to the dumb creatures.

The night was a beautiful one; the moon was better than a quarter old; and Mick, looking up at her, could not help bestowing a blessing on her beautiful face, shining down so sweetly upon the gentle Awbeg. He had now got out of the open road and had come to where the trees grew on each side of it: he proceeded for some space in the half-and-half light which the moon gave through them. At one time when a big old tree got between him and the moon, it was so dark that he could hardly see the horse's head; then, as he passed on, the moonbeams would stream through the open boughs and variegate the road with lights and shades. Mick was lying down in the car at his ease, having got clear of the plantation, and was watching the bright piece of a moon in a little pool at the road side, when he saw it disappear all of a sudden as if a great cloud came over the sky. He turned round on his elbow to see if it was so, but how was Mick astonished at finding, close along-side of the car, a great high black coach drawn by six black horses, with long black tails reaching almost down to the ground, and a coachman dressed all in black sitting up on the box. But what surprised Mick the most was, that he could see no sign of a head either upon coachman or horses. It swept rapidly by him, and he could perceive the horses raising their feet as if they were in a fine slinging trot, the coachman touching them up with his long whip, and the wheels spinning round like hoddy-doddies; still he could hear no noise, only the regular step of his gossip Darby's horse, and the squeaking of the gudgeons of the car, that were as good as lost entirely for want of a little grease.

Poor Mick's heart almost died within him, but he said nothing, only looked on; and the black coach swept away, and was soon lost among some distant trees. Mick saw nothing more of it, or indeed of any thing else. He got home just as the moon was going down behind Mount Hillery—took the tackling off the horse, turned the beast out in the field for the night, and got to his bed.

Next morning, early, he was standing at the road-side thinking of all that had happened the night before, when he saw Dan Madden, that was Mr. Wrixon's huntsman, coming on the master's best horse down the hill, as hard as ever he went at the tail of the hounds. Mick's mind instantly misgave him that all was not right, so he stood out in the very middle of the road, and caught hold of Dan's bridle when he came up.

"Mick, dear—for the love of God! don't stop me," cried Dan.

"Why, what's the hurry?" said Mick.

"Oh, the master!—he's off—he's off—he'll never cross a horse again till the day of judgment!"

"Why, what would ail his honour?" said Mick; "sure it is no later than yesterday morning that I was talking to him, and he stout and hearty; and says he to me, Mick, says he"—

"Stout and hearty was he?" answered Madden; "and was he not out with me in the kennel last night, when I was feeding the dogs; and didn't he come out to the stable, and give a ball to Peg Pullaway with his own hand, and tell me he'd ride the old General to-day; and sure," said Dan, wiping his eyes with the sleeve of his coat, "who'd have thought that the first thing I'd see this morning was the mistress standing at my bed-side, and bidding me get up and ride off like fire for Doctor Johnson; for the master had got a fit, and"—poor Dan's grief choked his voice—"oh, Mick! if you have a heart in you, run over yourself, or send the gessoon for Kate Finnigan, the midwife; she's a cruel skilful woman, and maybe she might save the master, till I get the doctor."

Dan struck his spurs into the hunter, and Michael Noonan flung off his newly-mended brogues, and cut across the fields to Kate Finnigan's; but neither the doctor nor Katty was of any avail, and the next night's moon saw Ballygibblin—and more's the pity—a house of mourning.

To an anonymous correspondent (A. H. B. Clonmel) the compiler is chiefly indebted for the foregoing legend. Burke's residence in the neighbourhood of, and early education at Castletown roche, are noticed by Mr. Prior in his excellent life of that illustrious man.

Another legend of the same district relates, that a black coach, drawn by headless horses, goes every night from Castle Hyde till it comes to Glana Fauna, a little beyond Ballyhooly, when it proceeds up the valley, and then returns back again. The same coach is also reported to drive every Saturday night through the town of Doneraile, and to stop at the doors of different houses; but should any one be so fool-hardy as to open the door, a basin of blood is instantly flung in their face.

The appearance of "the Headless Coach," as it is called, is a very general superstition, and is generally regarded as a sign of death, or an omen of some misfortune.

" The people of Basse Bretagne believe, that when the death of any person is at hand, a hearse drawn by skeletons (which they call *carriquet an nankon*), and covered with a white sheet, passes by the house where the sick person lies, and the creaking of the wheels may be plainly heard."—*Journal des Sciences, 1826, communicated by Dr. Grimm.*

The Glasgow Chronicle (January, 1826) records the following occurrence at Paisley, on the occasion of some silkweavers being out of employment.

"Visions have been seen of carts, caravans, and coaches going up Gleniffer braes without horses, or with horses without heads. Not many nights ago, mourning coaches, too, were seen going up the Cart above the town, with all the solemnity of a funeral. Some hoary-headed citizens relate, that about thirty years backward in their history, a famine was prognosticated in much the same way, by unusual appearances in the Causey-side. The most formidable witnesses in favour of the visions come from Neilston, who declare that they have seen the coaches, &c. two by two, coming over the braes, and are quite willing to depose to said facts whenever asked, before the Paisley magistrates."

Places where any fatal accident has occurred, or any murder been committed, are seldom without a supernatural tale of terror, in which the headless coach and horses perform their part. One instance will probably suffice.

Many years ago, a clergyman belonging to St. Catharine's church in Dublin resided at the old castle of Donore, in the vicinity of that city. From melancholy, or some other cause, he put an end to his existence, by hanging himself out of a window near the top of the castle, so small that it was matter of surprise how he was able to force his body through it.

That he had supernatural aid in accomplishing the deed is the belief of the neighbourhood; for, besides the smallness of the window, there is the farther evidence that, to this very day, the mark of his figure is seen on the wall beneath it, and no whitewashing is able to efface it. After his death, a coach, sometimes driven by a coachman without a head, sometimes drawn by horses without heads, was frequently observed at night driving furiously by Roper's Rest, so the castle was called from him.

Popular legends are full of accounts of wild huntsmen, and such restless personages. King Arthur, we are told, used to hunt in the English woods: no one could see the monarch himself, but the sounding of the horns and the cry of the hounds might be plainly heard; and when any one called out after him, an answer was returned—"We are king Arthur and his kindred." In France there was Le Grand Veneur, who haunted the woods round Fontainebleau; in Germany, Hackelberg, who gave up his share of heaven for permission to hunt till doomsday; in Sleswick, king Abel; in the Danish islands, Græn Jette, who rides with his head under his arm; Palna Jäger, and king Wolmar, or Waldemar: this last monarch also hunts in Jutland, where he may be heard continually crying out, *Hei! Hou! Lystig! Courage!* which are the names of his four hounds. For hunting fairies, see Waldron, p. 132; also Cromek's Remains of Nithisdale and Galloway Song, p. 298, and note on subsequent story.

THE HARVEST DINNER.

It was Monday, and a fine October morning. The sun had been some time above the mountains, and the hoar frost and the drops on the gossamers were glittering in the light, when Thady Byrne, on coming in to get his breakfast, after having dug out a good piece of his potatoes, saw his neighbour, Paddy Cavenagh, who lived on the other side of the road, at his own door tying his brogues.

"A good morrow to you, Paddy, honey," said Thady Byrne.

"Good morrow, kindly, Thady," said Paddy.

"Why then, Paddy avick, it is not your early rising, any how, that will do you any harm this morning."

"It 's true enough for you, Thady," answered Paddy, casting a look up at the sky; "for I believe it 's pretty late in the day. But I was up, you see, murdering late last night."

"To be sure, then, Paddy, it was up at the great dinner, yesterday, above at the big house you were."

"Ay was it; and a rattling fine dinner we had of it, too."

"Why, then, Paddy, agrah, what is to ail you now, but you 'd just sit yourself down here, on this piece of green sod, and tell us all about it, from beginning to end."

"Never say the word twice, man; I 'll give you the whole full and true account of it, and welcome."

They sat down on the road side, and Paddy thus began:

"Well, you see, Thady, we 'd a powerful great harvest of it, you know, this year, and the men all worked like jewels as they are; and the master was in great spirits, and he promised he 'd give us all a grand dinner when the drawing-in was over, and the corn all safe in the haggard. So this last week crowned the business; and on Saturday night the last sheaf was neatly tied and sent in to the mistress, and every thing was finished, all to the thatching of the ricks. Well, you see, just as Larry Toole was come down from heading the last rick, and we were taking away the ladder, out comes the mistress, herself—long life to her—by the light of the moon; and 'Boys,' says she, 'yez have finished the harvest bravely, and I invite yez all to dinner here, to-morrow; and if yez come early, yez shall have mass in the big hall, without the trouble of going up all the ways to the chapel for it.' "

"Why, then, did she really say so, Paddy?"

"That she did—the sorrow the lie in it."

"Well, go on."

"Well, if we did not set up a shout for her, it 's no matter!"

"Ay, and good right you had too, Paddy, avick."

"Well, you see, yesterday morning—which, God be praised! was as fine a day as ever came out of the sky—when I had taken the beard off me, Tom Connor and I set out for the big house. And I don't know, Thady, whether it was the fineness of the day, or the thoughts of the good dinner we were to have, or the kindness of the mistress, that made my heart so light, but I felt, anyhow, as gay as any sky-lark.—Well, when we got up to the house, there was every one of the people that 's in the work, men, women, and childer, all come together in the yard; and a pretty sight it was to look upon, Thady—they were all so gay, and so clean, and so happy."

"True for you, Paddy, agrah; and a fine thing it is, too, to work with a real gentleman, like the master. But tell us, avick, how it was the mistress contrived to get the mass for yez:

sure father Clancey, himself, or the coadjutor, didn't come over?"

"No, in troth didn't they; but the mistress managed it better nor all that. You see, Thady, there's a priest, an old friend of the family's, one father Mullin, on a visit this fortnight past, up at the big house. He's as gay a little man as ever spoke, only he's a little too fond of the drop—the more is the pity—and it's whispered about among the servants, that by means of it he has lost a parish he had down the country; and he was on his way up to Dublin, when he stopped to spend a few days with his old friends, the master and mistress.

"Well, you see, the mistress, on Saturday, without saying a single word of it to any living soul, writes a letter with her own hand, and sends Tom Freen off with it to father Clancey, to ax him for a loan of the vestments. Father Clancey, you know, is a mighty *genteel* man, and one that likes to oblige the quality in any thing that does not go against his duty; and glad he was to have it in his power to serve the mistress; and he sent off the vestments with all his heart and soul, and as civil a letter, Tommy Freen says—for he heard the mistress reading it—as ever was penned.

"Well, there was an altar, you see, got up in the big hall, just between the two doors—if ever you were in it—leading into the store-room and the room the childer sleep in; and when every thing was ready we all came in, and the priest gave us as good mass every bit as if we were up at the chapel for it. The mistress and all the family attended themselves, and they stood just within-side of the parlour-door; and it was really surprising, Thady, to see how decently they behaved themselves. If they 'd been all their lives going to chapel they could not have behaved themselves better nor they did."

"Ay, Paddy, mavourneen, I 'll be bail they didn't skit and laugh the way some people would be doing."

"Laugh!—not themselves, indeed! They 'd more manners, if nothing else, nor to do that.—Well, to go on with my story: when the mass was over we went strolling about the lawn and place till three o'clock come, and then, you see, the big bell rung out for dinner, and maybe it was not we that were glad to hear it. So away with us to the long barn where the dinner was laid out; and upon my conscience, Thady Byrne, there 's not one word of lie in what I 'm going to tell you; but at the sight of so much victuals every taste of appetite in the world left me, and I thought I 'd have fainted down on the ground that was under me. There was, you see, two rows of long tables laid the whole length of the barn, and table-cloths spread upon every inch of them; and there was rounds of beef, and rumps of beef, and ribs of beef, both boiled and roast; and there was legs of mutton, and hands of pork, and pieces of fine bacon; and there was cabbage and potatoes to no end, and a knife and fork laid for every body; and barrels of beer and porter, with the cocks in every one of them, and mugs and porringers in heaps. In all my born days, Thady dear, I never laid eyes on such a load of victuals."

"By the powers of delph! Paddy ahayger, and it *was* a grand sight sure enough. Tear and ayjers! what ill luck I had not to be in the work this year! But go on, agrah."

"Well, you see, the master, himself, stood up at the end of one of the tables, and cut up a fine piece of the beef for us; and right forenent him sat, at the other end, old Paddy Byrne; for, though you know he is a farmer himself, yet the mistress is so fond of him—he is such a decent man—that she would, by all manner of means, have him there. Then the priest was at the head of the other table, and said grace for us, and then fell to slashing up another piece of the beef for us; and forenent him sat Jem Murray the stewart; and sure enough, Thady, it was ourselves that played away in grand style at the beef, and the mutton, and the cabbage, and all the other fine things. And there was Tom Freen, and all the other servants waiting upon us, and handing us drink, just as if we were so many grand gentlemen that were dining with the master.—Well, you see, when we were about half done, in walks the mistress herself, and the young master, and the young ladies, and the ladies from Dublin that 's down on a visit with the mistress, just, as she said, to see if we were happy and merry over our dinner; and then, Thady, you see, without any body saying a single word, we all stood up like one man, and every man and boy, with his full porringer of porter in his hand, drank long life and success to the mistress and master, and every one of the family.—I don't know for others, Thady, but for myself, I never said a prayer in all my life more from the heart; and a good right I had, sure, and every one that was there, too; for, to say nothing of the dinner, is there the like of her in the whole side of the country for goodness to the poor, whether they 're sick or they 're well? Would not I myself, if it was not but for her, be a lone and desolate man this blessed day?"

"It 's true for you, avick, for she brought Judy through it better nor any doctor of them all."

"Well, to make a long story short, we ate and

we drank, and we talked and we laughed, till we were tired, and as soon as it grew dusk we were all called again into the hall; and there, you see, the mistress had got over Tim Connel, the blind piper, and had sent for all the women that could come, and the cook had tea for them down below in the kitchen; and they came up to the hall, and there was chairs set round it for us all to sit upon, and the mistress came out of the parlour, and 'Boys,' says she, 'I hope yez have made a good dinner, and I've been thinking of yez, you see, and I've got yez plenty of partners, and it's your own faults if yez don't spend a pleasant evening.' So with that we set up another shout for the mistress, and Tim struck up, and the master took out Nelly Mooney into the middle of the floor to dance a jig, and it was they that footed it neatly. Then the master called out Dinny Moran, and dragged him up to one of the Dublin young ladies, and bid Dinny be stout and ax her out to dance with him. So Dinny, you see, though he was ashamed to make so free with the lady, still he was afeard not to do as the master bid him; so, by my conscience, he bowled up to her manfully, and held out the fist and axed her out to dance with him, and she gave him her hand in a crack, and Dinny whipped her out into the middle of the hall, forenent us all, and pulled up his breeches, and called out to Tim to blow up 'The Rocks of Cashel' for them. And then, my jewel, if you were to see them! Dinny flinging the legs about as if they'd fly from off him, and the lady now here now there, just for all the world as if she was a spirit, for not a taste of noise did she make on the floor that ever was heard; and Dinny calling out to Tim to play it up faster and faster, and Tim almost working his elbow through the bag, till at last the lady was fairly tired, and Dinny clapped his hands and called out Peggy Reilly, and she attacked him boldly, and danced down Dinny, and then up got Johnny Regan, and put her down completely. And since the world was a world, I believe there never was such dancing seen."

"The sorrow the doubt of it, avick, I'm certain; they're all of them such real fine dancers. And only to think of the lady dancing with the likes of Dinny!"

"Well, you see, poor old Paddy Byrne, when he hears that the women were all to be there, in he goes into the parlour to the mistress, and axes her if he might make so bold as to go home and fetch his woman. So the mistress, you see—though you know Katty Byrne is no great favourite with her—was glad to oblige Paddy, and so Katty Byrne was there too. And then old

Hugh Carr axed her out to move a *minnet* with him; and there was Hugh, as stiff as if he had dined upon one of the spits, with his black wig and his long brown coat, and his blue stockings, moving about with his hat in his hand, and leading Katty about, and looking so soft upon her; and Katty, in her stiff mob-cap, with the ears pinned down under her chin, and her little black hat on the top of her head; and she at one corner *curcheying* to Hugh, and Hugh at another bowing to her, and every body wondering at them, they moved it so elegantly."

"Troth, Paddy, avourneen, that was well worth going a mile of ground to see."

"Well, you see, when the dancing was over, they took to the singing, and Bill Carey gave the 'Wounded Hussar' and the 'Poor but Honest Soldier' in such style, that you 'd have heard him up on the top of Slee Roo; and Dinny Moran and old Tom Freen gave us the best songs they had, and the priest sung the Cruiskeen Laun for us gaily, and one of the young ladies played and sung upon a thing within in the parlour like a table, that was prettier nor any pipes to listen to."

"And didn't Bill give yez 'As down by Banna's banks I strayed?' Sure that 's one of the best songs he has."

"And that he did, till he made the very seats

shake under us; but a body can't remember every thing, you know. Well, where was I?—oh, ay! —You see, my dear, the poor little priest was all the night long going backwards and forwards, every minute, between the parlour and the hall, and the spirits, you see, was lying open upon the sideboard, and the dear little man he couldn't keep himself from it, but kept helping himself to a drop now and a drop then, till at last he became all as one as tipsy. So, then, he comes out into the hall among us, and goes about whispering to us to go home, and not be keeping the family out of their beds. But the mistress saw what he was at, and she spoke out, and she said, 'Good people,' says she, 'never mind what the priest says to yez —yez are my company, and not his, and yez are heartily welcome to stay as long as yez like.' So when he found he could get no good of us, he rolled off with himself to his bed; and his head, you see, was so bothered with the liquor he'd been taking that he never once thought of taking off his boots, but tumbled into bed with them upon him—Tommy Freen told us when he went into the room to look after him; and devil be in Tim, when he heard it, but he lilts up the 'Priest in his boots;' and, God forgive us! we all burst out laughing; for sure who could help it, if it was the bishop himself?"

"Troth it was a shame for yez, anyhow. But Paddy, agrah, did yez come away at all?"

"Why at last we did, after another round of punch to the glory and success of the family. And now, Thady, comes the most surprisingest part of the whole story. I was all alone, you see; for my woman, you know, could not leave the childer to come to the dance, so, as it was a fine moonshiny night, nothing would do me but I must go out into the paddock to look after poor Rainbow, the plough-bullock, that has got a bad shoulder; so by that means, you see, I missed the company, and had to go home all alone. Well, you see, it was out by the back gate I went, and it was then about twelve in the night, as well as I could judge by the plough, and the moon was shining as bright as a silver dish, and there was not a sound to be heard but the screeching of the old owl down in the ivy-wall; and I felt it all pleasant, for I was somehow rather hearty with the drink I'd been taking; for you know, Thady Byrne, I'm a sober man."

"That's no lie for you, Paddy, avick. A little, as they say, goes a great way with you."

"Well, you see, on I went whistling to myself some of the tunes they'd been singing, and thinking of any thing, sure, but the good people; when just as I came to the corner of the plantation, and got a sight of the big bush, I thought, faith, I saw some things moving backwards and forwards, and dancing like, up in the bush. I was quite certain it was the fairies that, you know, resort to it, for I could see, I thought, their little red caps and green jackets quite plain. Well, I was thinking at first of going back and getting home through the fields: but, says I to myself, what should I be afeard of? I'm an honest man, says I, that does nobody any harm; and I heard mass this morning; and it's neither Hollyeve, nor St. John's eve, nor any other of their great days, and they can do me no hurt, I'm certain. So I made the sign of the cross, and on I went in God's name, till I came right under the bush; and what do you think they were, Thady, after all?"

"Arrah, how can I tell? But you were a stout man anyhow, Paddy, agrah!"

"Why then, what was it but the green leaves of the old bush and the red bunches of the haws that were waving and shaking in the moonlight. Well, on I goes till I came to the corner of the crab-road, when I happened to cast my eyes over towards the little moat that is in the moat-field, and there, by my *sowl!* (God forgive me for swearing) I saw the fairies in real earnest."

"You did, then, did you?"

"Ay, by my faith, did I, and a mighty pretty

sight it was too, I can tell you. The side of the moat, you see, that looks into the field was open, and out of it there came the darlintest little cavalcade of the prettiest little fellows you ever laid your eyes upon. They were all dressed in green hunting frocks, with nice little red caps on their heads, and they were mounted on pretty little long-tailed white ponies, not so big as young kids, and they rode two and two so nicely. Well, you see, they took right across the field just above the sand-pit, and I was wondering in myself what they'd do when they came to the big ditch, thinking they'd never get over it. But I'll tell you what it is, Thady,—Mr. Tom and the brown mare, though they're both of them gay good at either ditch or wall, they're not to be talked of in the same day with them. They took the ditch, you see, big as it is, in full stroke; not a man of them was shook in his seat or lost his rank; it was pop, pop, pop, over with them, and then, hurra!—away with them like shot across the high field, in thie direction of the old church.

Well, my dear, while I was straining my eyes looking after, I hears a great rumbling noise coming out of the moat, and when I turned about to look at it, what should I see but a great old family coach and six coming out of the moat and making direct for the gate where I was standing. Well, says I,

I 'm a lost man now anyhow. There was no use at all, you see, in thinking to run for it, for they were driving at the rate of a hunt ; so down I got into the gripe, thinking to sneak off with myself while they were opening the gate. But, by the laws! the gate flew open without a soul laying a finger to it, the instant minute they came up to it, and they wheeled down the road just close to the spot where I was hiding, and I saw them as plain as I now see you ; and a queer sight it was, too, to see, for not a morsel of head that ever was, was there upon one of the horses or on the coachman either, and yet, for all that, Thady, the lord *Léffenent*'s coach could not have made a handier or a shorter turn nor they did out of the gate ; and the blind thief of a coachman, just as they were making the wheel, was near taking the eye out of me with the lash of his long whip, as he was cutting up the horses to show off his driving. I 've my doubts that the schemer knew I was there well enough, and that he did it all on purpose. Well, as it passed by me, I peeped in at the quality within-side, and not a head, no not as big as the head of a pin, was there among the whole kit of them, and four fine footmen that were standing behind the coach were just like the rest of them."

"Well, to be sure, but it was a queer sight."

"Well, away they went tattering along the

road, making the fire fly out of the stones at no rate. So when I saw they'd no eyes, I knew it was *un*possible they could ever see me, so up I got out of the ditch and after them with me along the road as hard as ever I could drive. But when I got to the rise of the hill I saw they were a great way a-head of me, and had taken to the fields, and were making off for the old church too. I thought they might have some business of their own there, and that it might not be safe for strangers to be going after them; so as I was by this time near my own house, I went in and got quietly to bed without saying any thing to the woman about it; and long enough it was before I could get to sleep for thinking of them, and that's the reason, Thady, I was up so late this morning. But was not it a strange thing, Thady?"

"Faith, and sure it was, Paddy, ahayger, as strange a thing as ever was. But are you quite certain and sure now you saw them?"

"Am I certain and sure I saw them? Am I certain and sure I see the nose there on your face? What was to ail me not to see them? Was not the moon shining as bright as day? And did not they pass within a yard of where I was? And did any one ever see me drunk or hear me tell a lie?"

"It's true for you, Paddy, no one ever did, and myself does not rightly know what to say to it."

The scene of the Harvest Dinner lies in Leinster; and the nice observer will perceive some slight differences between the language in it, and the Munster dialect of the other tales. At the end of "the drawing-in," a sheaf very neatly bound up is sent in to "the mistress," a symbol of the termination of her harvest cares: as a matter of course, the bearer "gets a glass" to drink her health, and a general invitation to "the people in the work" follows.

Gossamers, a word used in the opening, Johnson says, are the long white cobwebs which fly in the air in calm sunny weather, and he derives the word from the low Latin gossapium. This is altogether very unsatisfactory. The gossamers are the cobwebs which may be seen, particularly during a still autumnal morning, in such quantities on the furze bushes, and which are raised by the wind and floated through the air, as thus exquisitely pictured by Browne in Britannia's Pastorals:

> "The milk-white gossamers not upwards snowed."
>
> Book II. Song 2.

Every lover of nature must have observed and admired the beautiful appearance of the gossamers in the early morning, when covered with dew-drops, which, like prisms, separate the rays of light, and shoot the blue, red, yellow, and other colours of the spectrum, in brilliant confusion. Of king Oberon we are told—

> " A rich mantle he did wear,
> Made of tinsel gossamer,
> Bestarred over with a few
> Diamond drops of morning dew."

The word gossamer is evidently derived from *goss*, the gorse or furze. Query, *Goss samyt?* Voss, in a note to Luise, III. 17, says, that in Germany the popular belief attributes the manufacture of the gossamer to the dwarfs and elves.

There is something peculiarly pleasing in the terms of affection used by the lower orders of the Irish in addressing each other; the expressions, *agrah* (my love) and *avick* (my son) resemble the *hijos* and *humanos* of the Spaniards, and the *fathers* and *sons* of the Hebrews and Arabs. It is curious that this orientalism, if it may be called such, should be only found in Spain and Ireland. Perhaps its common origin lies in warmth of affection, of which no country affords more instances than the one last mentioned. On turning over the unhappily too dark pages of Irish history, the reader must be struck with meeting, in the space of one reign, the deaths of no less than three persons ascribed to grief for the loss of friends. One is an earl of Kildare, who, we are told, pined and died when death deprived him of his foster brother. The cause assigned may not be the true one, but the bond of affection must have been strong in a country where such could even be mentioned. Golownin gives an instance of nearly similar strength of affection among the Japanese.

The perfection of singing, in the opinion of an Irish peasant, consists in strength of lungs. "A powerful bass voice that could be heard at the top of a neighbouring mountain," carries off the palm of excellence, and is sought after and listened to with enthusiasm. The favourite songs display no mean degree of popular taste. Campbell's beautiful and pathetic ballad, mentioned in the tale, is an especial favourite; and "Adelaide," and "the dark-rolling Danube," are as familiar to the ears of the Irish peasantry as Ogle's "Molly Asthore," and "Banna's banks." As a further proof of their natural good taste, it may be mentioned, that of the books printed and circulated by the Kildare Street Society, none is found to equal in sale Elizabeth, or the Exiles of Siberia. The reader will probably call to mind Gilbert Burns' remarks on the kindred taste of the Scottish peasantry. Much may be said respecting educating the lower orders, according to their taste and through the medium of their superstitions, as the most attractive and effectual modes of instruction. But the great question of national education is one of too much importance to be trifled with in a hastily written note.

The appearance of the fairy hunters has some resemblance to the relation in M'Culloch's account of the Highlands and Western Isles of Scotland,' vol. iv. p. 358. "One Highlander, in passing a mountain, hears the tramp of horses, the music of the horn, and the cheering of the huntsman; when suddenly a gallant crew of thirteen fairy hunters, dressed in green, sweep by him, the silver bosses of their bridles jingling in the night breeze."

The subsequent attested statement has been transmitted to the writer from Ireland, among other intelligence of fairy proceedings there.

"The accuracy of the following story I can vouch for, having heard it told several times by the person who saw the circumstances.

"'About twenty years back William Cody, churnboy to a person near Cork, had, after finishing his day's work, to go through six or eight fields to his own house, about 12 o'clock at night. He was passing alongside of the ditch (Anglicè, hedge) of a large field, and coming near a quarry, he heard a great cracking of whips at the other side; he went on to a gap in the same ditch, and out rode a little horseman, dressed in green, and mounted in the best manner, who put a whip to his breast and made him stop until several hundred horseman, all dressed alike, rode out of the gap at full speed, and swept round a glin: when the last horseman was clear off, the sentinel clapt spurs to his horse, gave three cracks of his whip, and was out of sight in a second.'

"The person would swear to the above, as he was quite sober and sensible at the time. The place had always before the name of being very airy *."

(*Signed*) P. Bath,
Royal Cork Institution, 3d June, 1825.

* A lonesome place, in Scotland and Ireland, is commonly said to be "an airy place," from *airidhe*, which in Irish signifies spectres, visions.

Sir Walter Scott, in Minstrelsy of Scottish Border, vol. ii. explains this word "as producing superstitious dread."

In the ballad of Tamlane we find

"Gloomy, gloomy was the night,
And *eiry* was the way," &c.

THE DEATH COACH.

'Tis midnight!—how gloomy and dark!
By Jupiter there's not a star!—
'Tis fearful!—'tis awful!—and hark!
What sound is that comes from afar?

Still rolling and rumbling, that sound
Makes nearer and nearer approach;
Do I tremble, or is it the ground?—
Lord save us!—what is it?—a coach!—

A coach!—but that coach has no head;
And the horses are headless as it;
Of the driver the same may be said,
And the passengers inside who sit.

See the wheels! how they fly o'er the stones!
And whirl, as the whip it goes crack:
Their spokes are of dead men's thigh bones,
And the pole is the spine of the back!

The hammer-cloth, shabby display,
  Is a pall rather mildew'd by damps;
And to light this strange coach on its way,
  Two hollow skulls hang up for lamps!

From the gloom of Rathcooney church-yard,
  They dash down the hill of Glanmire;
Pass Lota in gallop as hard
  As if horses were never to tire!

With people thus headless 'tis fun
  To drive in such furious career;
Since *headlong* their horses can't run,
  Nor coachman be *headdy* from beer.

Very steep is the Tivoli lane,
  But up-hill to them is as down;
Nor the charms of Woodhill can detain
  These Dullahans rushing to town.

Could they feel as I 've felt—in a song—
  A spell that forbade them depart;
They 'd a lingering visit prolong,
  And after their head lose their heart!

No matter!—'tis past twelve o'clock;
  Through the streets they sweep on like the
    wind,

And, taking the road to Blackrock,
Cork city is soon left behind.

Should they hurry thus reckless along,
To supper instead of to bed,
The landlord will surely be wrong,
If he charge it at so much a head !

Yet mine host may suppose them too poor
To bring to his wealth an increase ;
As till now, all who drove to his door,
Possess'd at least *one crown* a-piece.

Up the Deadwoman's hill they are roll'd ;
Boreenmannah is quite out of sight ;
Ballintemple they reach, and behold !
At its church-yard they stop and alight.

" Who 's there ?" said a voice from the ground ;
" We 've no room, for the place is quite full."
" O room must be speedily found,
For we come from the parish of Skull.

" Though Murphys and Crowleys appear
On headstones of deep-letter'd pride ;
Though Scannels and Murleys lie here,
Fitzgeralds and Toomies beside ;

"Yet here for the night we lie down,
To-morrow we speed on the gale;
For having no heads of our own,
We seek the Old Head of Kinsale."

The Death Coach is called in Irish "*Coach a bower.*" The time of its appearance is always midnight; and when heard to drive round any particular house, with the coachman's whip cracking loudly, it is said to be a sure omen of death.

The following account of the Dullahans and their coach was communicated to the writer by a lady resident in the neighbourhood of Cork:—

"They drive particularly hard wherever a death is going to take place. The people about here thought that the road would be completely worn out with their galloping before Mrs. Spiers died. On the night the poor lady departed they brought an immense procession with them, and instead of going up the road, as usual, they turned into Tivoli: the lodge-people, according to their own account, 'were *kilt* from them that night.' The coachman has a most marvellously long whip, with which he can whip the eyes out of any one, at any distance, that dares to look at him. I suppose the reason he is so incensed at being looked at, is because he cannot return the compliment, '*pon the 'count* of having no head. What a pity it is none but the Dullahans can go without their heads! Some people's heads would be no loss to them, or any one else."

A like superstition to the circumstance of "whipping out the eyes," is related by Mr. Thiele as current in Denmark. He tells us, that the oppressive lords of Glorup drive every Christmas night, in a stately coach, from their magnificent tomb in St. Knud's church, in Odense, to Glorup. The coach is drawn by six white horses, with long glowing tongues; and he who dares not hide his face when he hears it coming, atones for his rashness with loss of sight.

Danske Folkesagn, vol. ii. p. 104.

"I cannot find," says a fair Welsh correspondent, "that we have any peculiar designation for the headless people beyond "*Fenyw heb un pen*," the headless woman—"*Ceffyl heb un pen*," the headless horse; further we have not aspired, nor have I heard that this headless race in Wales extends beyond an humble horse. With us they have not assumed the same importance as in Ireland, by setting up their carriage."

The localities mentioned in the verses are all in the immediate vicinity of the city of Cork, with the exception of Skull and the Old Head of Kinsale, both of which lie on the coast of that county.

THE HEADLESS HORSEMAN.

"God speed you, and a safe journey this night to you, Charley," ejaculated the master of the little sheebeen house at Ballyhooley after his old friend and good customer, Charley Culnane, who at length had turned his face homewards, with the prospect of as dreary a ride and as dark a night as ever fell upon the Blackwater, along whose banks he was about to journey.

Charley Culnane knew the country well, and, moreover, was as bold a rider as any Mallow-boy that ever *rattled* a four-year-old upon Drumrue race-course. He had gone to Fermoy in the morning, as well for the purpose of purchasing some ingredients required for the Christmas dinner by his wife, as to gratify his own vanity by having new reins fitted to his snaffle, in which he intended showing off the old mare at the approaching St. Stephen's day hunt.

Charley did not get out of Fermoy until late; for although he was not one of your "nasty particular sort of fellows" in any thing that related to the common occurrences of life, yet in all the appointments connected with hunting, riding, leaping, in short, in whatever was connected with the old mare, "Charley," the saddlers said, "was the devil to *plăse*." An illustration of this fastidiousness was afforded by his going such a distance for a snaffle bridle. Mallow was full twelve miles nearer Charley's farm (which lay just three quarters of a mile below Carrick) than Fermoy; but Charley had quarrelled with all the Mallow saddlers, from hard-working and hard-drinking Tim Clancey, up to Mister Ryan, who wrote himself "Saddler to the Duhallow Hunt;" and no one could content him in all particulars but honest Michael Twomey of Fermoy, who used to assert —and who will doubt it?—that he could stitch a saddle better than the lord-lieutenant, although they made him all as one as king over Ireland.

This delay in the arrangement of the snaffle bridle did not allow Charley Culnane to pay so long a visit as he had at first intended to his old friend and gossip, Con Buckley, of the "Harp of Erin." Con, however, knew the value of time, and insisted upon Charley making good use of what he had to spare. "I won't bother you waiting for water, Charley, because I think you 'll have enough of that same before you get home; so drink off your liquor, man. It 's as good *parlia-*

ment as ever a gentleman tasted, ay, and holy church to, for it will bear "x *waters*," and carry the bead after that, may be."

Charley, it must be confessed, nothing loth, drank success to Con, and success to the jolly "Harp of Erin," with its head of beauty and its strings of the hair of gold, and to their better acquaintance, and so on, from the bottom of his soul, until the bottom of the bottle reminded him that Carrick was at the bottom of the hill on the other side of Castletown Roche, and that he had got no further on his journey than his gossip's at Ballyhooley, close to the big gate of Convamore. Catching hold of his oil-skin hat, therefore, whilst Con Buckley went to the cupboard for another bottle of "the real stuff," he regularly, as it is termed, bolted from his friend's hospitality, darted to the stable, tightened his girths, and put the old mare into a canter towards home.

The road from Ballyhooley to Carrick follows pretty nearly the course of the Blackwater, occasionally diverging from the river and passing through rather wild scenery, when contrasted with the beautiful seats that adorn its banks. Charley cantered gaily, regardless of the rain which, as his friend Con had anticipated, fell in torrents: the good woman's currants and raisins were carefully packed between the folds of his yeomanry cloak, which Charley, who was proud of showing that he belonged to the "Royal Mallow Light Horse Volunteers," always strapped to the saddle before him, and took care never to destroy the military effect of by putting it on.—Away he went singing like a thrush—

"Sporting, belling, dancing, drinking,
Breaking windows—(*hiccup!*)—sinking;
Ever raking—never thinking,
Live the rakes of Mallow.

"Spending faster than it comes,
Beating—(*hiccup*, *hic*), and duns,
Duhallow's true-begotten sons,
Live the rakes of Mallow."

Notwithstanding that the visit to the jolly "Harp of Erin" had a little increased the natural complacency of his mind, the drenching of the new snaffle reins began to disturb him; and then followed a train of more anxious thoughts than even were occasioned by the dreaded defeat of the pride of his long-anticipated *turn out* on St. Stephen's day. In an hour of good fellowship, when his heart was warm, and his head not over cool, Charley had backed the old mare against Mr. Jepson's bay filly Desdemona for a neat hundred, and he now felt sore misgivings as to the prudence of the match. In a less gay tone he continued

> "Living short, but merry lives,
> Going where the devil drives,
> Keeping———"

"Keeping" he muttered, as the old mare had reduced her canter to a trot at the bottom of Kilcummer Hill. Charley's eye fell on the old walls that belonged, in former times, to the Templars; but the silent gloom of the ruin was broken only by the heavy rain which splashed and pattered on the gravestones. He then looked up at the sky to see if there was, among the clouds, any hopes for mercy on his new snaffle reins; and no sooner were his eyes lowered, than his attention was arrested by an object so extraordinary as almost led him to doubt the evidence of his senses. The head, apparently, of a white horse, with short cropped ears, large open nostrils, and immense eyes, seemed rapidly to follow him. No connexion with body, legs, or rider, could possibly be traced—the head advanced—Charley's old mare, too, was moved at this unnatural sight, and, snorting violently, increased her trot up the hill. The head moved forward, and passed on;

Charley pursuing it with astonished gaze, and wondering by what means, and for what purpose, this detached head thus proceeded through the air, did not perceive the corresponding body until he was suddenly started by finding it close at his side. Charley turned to examine what was thus so sociably jogging on with him, when a most unexampled apparition presented itself to his view. A figure, whose height (judging as well as the obscurity of the night would permit him) he computed to be at least eight feet, was seated on the body and legs of a white horse full eighteen hands and a half high. In this measurement Charley could not be mistaken, for his own mare was exactly fifteen hands, and the body that thus jogged alongside he could at once determine, from his practice in horseflesh, was at least three hands and a half higher.

After the first feeling of astonishment, which found vent in the exclamation "I'm sold now for ever!" was over; the attention of Charley, being a keen sportsman, was naturally directed to this extraordinary body, and having examined it with the eye of a connoisseur, he proceeded to reconnoitre the figure so unusually mounted, who had hitherto remained perfectly mute. Wishing to see whether his companion's silence proceeded from bad temper, want of conversational powers, or from a distate to water, and the fear that the opening of his mouth might subject him to have it filled by the rain, which was then drifting in violent gusts against them, Charley endeavoured to catch a sight of his companion's face, in order to form an opinion on that point. But his vision failed in carrying him further than the top of the collar of the figure's coat, which was a scarlet single-breasted hunting frock, having a waist of a very old fashioned cut reaching to the saddle, with two huge shining buttons at about a yard distance behind. "I ought to see farther than this, too," thought Charley, "although he is mounted on his high horse, like my cousin Darby, who was made barony constable last week, unless 'tis Con's whiskey that has blinded me entirely." However, see further he could not, and after straining his eyes for a considerable time to no purpose, he exclaimed, with pure vexation, "By the big bridge of Mallow, it is no head at all he has!"

"Look again, Charley Culnane," said a hoarse voice, that seemed to proceed from under the right arm of the figure.

Charley did look again, and now in the proper place, for he clearly saw, under the aforesaid right arm, that head from which the voice had proceeded, and such a head no mortal ever saw before.

It looked like a large cream cheese hung round with black puddings: no speck of colour enlivened the ashy paleness of the depressed features; the skin lay stretched over the unearthly surface, almost like the parchment head of a drum. Two fiery eyes of prodigious circumference, with a strange and irregular motion, flashed like meteors upon Charley, and a mouth that reached from either extremity of two ears, which peeped forth from under a profusion of matted locks of lustreless blackness. This head, which the figure had evidently hitherto concealed from Charley's eyes, now burst upon his view in all its hideousness. Charley, although a lad of proverbial courage in the county Cork, yet could not but feel his nerves a little shaken by this unexpected visit from the headless horseman, whom he considered this figure doubtless must be. The cropped-eared head of the gigantic horse moved steadily forward, always keeping from six to eight yards in advance. The horseman, unaided by whip or spur, and disdaining the use of stirrups, which dangled uselessly from the saddle, followed at a trot by Charley's side, his hideous head now lost behind the lappet of his coat, now starting forth in all its horror as the motion of the horse caused his arm to move to and fro. The ground shook under the weight of its supernatural burthen, and the water in the pools was agitated into waves as he trotted by them.

On they went—heads with bodies, and bodies without heads.—The deadly silence of night was broken only by the fearful clattering of hoofs, and the distant sound of thunder, which rumbled above the mystic hill of Cecaune a Mona Finnea. Charley, who was naturally a merry-hearted, and rather a talkative fellow, had hitherto felt tongue-tied by apprehension, but finding his companion showed no evil disposition towards him, and having become somewhat more reconciled to the Patagonian dimensions of the horseman and his headless steed, plucked up all his courage, and thus addressed the stranger—

"Why, then, your honour rides mighty well without the stirrups!"

"Humph," growled the head from under the horseman's right arm.

"'Tis not an over civil answer," thought Charley; "but no matter, he was taught in one of them riding-houses, may be, and thinks nothing at all about bumping his leather breeches at the rate of ten miles an hour. I'll try him on the other tack. Ahem!" said Charley, clearing his throat, and feeling at the same time rather daunted at this second attempt to establish a conversation. "Ahem! that's a mighty neat coat of your honour's, although 'tis a little too long in the waist for the present cut."

" Humph," growled again the head.

This second humph was a terrible thump in the face to poor Charley, who was fairly bothered to know what subject he could start that would prove more agreeable. " 'Tis a sensible head," thought Charley, " although an ugly one, for 'tis plain enough the man does not like flattery." A third attempt, however, Charley was determined to make, and having failed in his observations as to the riding and coat of his fellow-traveller, thought he would just drop a trifling allusion to the wonderful headless horse, that was jogging on so sociably beside his old mare; and as Charley was considered about Carrick to be very knowing in horses, besides being a full private in the Royal Mallow Light Horse Volunteers, which were every one of them mounted like real Hessians, he felt rather sanguine as to the result of his third attempt.

" To be sure, that 's a brave horse your honour rides," recommenced the persevering Charley.

" You may say that, with your own ugly mouth," growled the head.

Charley, though not much flattered by the compliment, nevertheless chuckled at his success in obtaining an answer, and thus continued:

"May be your honour wouldn't be after riding him across the country?"

"Will you try me, Charley?" said the head, with an inexpressible look of ghastly delight.

"Faith, and that 's what I 'd do," responded Charley, "only I 'm afraid, the night being so dark, of laming the old mare, and I 've every halfpenny of a hundred pounds on her heels."

This was true enough, Charley's courage was nothing dashed at the headless horseman's proposal; and there never was a steeple-chase, nor a fox-chase, riding or leaping in the country, that Charley Culnane was not at it, and foremost in it.

"Will you take my word," said the man who carried his head so snugly under his right arm, "for the safety of your mare?"

"Done," said Charley; and away they started, helter, skelter, over every thing, ditch and wall, pop, pop, the old mare never went in such style, even in broad daylight: and Charley had just the start of his companion, when the hoarse voice called out "Charley Culnane, Charley, man, stop for your life, stop!"

Charley pulled up hard. "Ay," said he, "you may beat me by the head, because it always goes so much before you; but if the bet was neck-and-neck, and that 's the go between the old mare and Desdemona, I 'd win it hollow!"

It appeared as if the stranger was well aware of what was passing in Charley's mind, for he suddenly broke out quite loquacious.

"Charley Culnane," says he, "you have a stout soul in you, and are every inch of you a good rider. I've tried you, and I ought to know; and that's the sort of man for my money. A hundred years it is since my horse and I broke our necks at the bottom of Kilcummer hill, and ever since I have been trying to get a man that dared to ride with me, and never found one before. Keep, as you have always done, at the tail of the hounds, never baulk a ditch, nor turn away from a stone wall, and the headless horseman will never desert you nor the old mare."

Charley, in amazement, looked towards the stranger's right arm, for the purpose of seeing in his face whether or not he was in earnest, but behold! the head was snugly lodged in the huge pocket of the horseman's scarlet hunting-coat. The horse's head had ascended perpendicularly above them, and his extraordinary companion rising quickly after his avant courier, vanished from the astonished gaze of Charley Culnane.

Charley, as may be supposed, was lost in wonder, delight, and perplexity; the pelting rain, the wife's pudding, the new snaffle—even the match against squire Jepson—all were forgotten; nothing could he think of, nothing could he talk of, but the headless horseman. He told it, directly that he got home, to Judy; he told it the following morning to all the neighbours; and he told it to the hunt on St. Stephen's day: but what provoked him after all the pains he took in describing the head, the horse, and the man, was, that one and all attributed the creation of the headless horseman to his friend Con Buckley's "X water parliament." This, however, should be told, that Charley's old mare beat Mr. Jepson's bay filly, Desdemona, by Diamond, and Charley pocketed his cool hundred; and if he didn't win by means of the headless horseman, I am sure I don't know any other reason for his doing so.

It has been already mentioned that Grœn Jette, the wild huntsman, usually rides with his head under his arm.

Cervantes mentions tales of the *Caballo sin cabeça* among the *cuentos de viejas con que se entretienen al fuego las dilatadas noches del invierno.* In the early part of the last century the headless horse was not unknown in England. The Spectator (No. 110) says —"My friend the butler desired me, with a very grave face, not to venture myself in it" (the wood), "after sunset, for that one of the footmen had been almost frightened out of his wits by a spirit that had appeared to him in the shape of a black horse without a head."

The horse, probably, like the dog, on account of our intimacy with him, is a favourite actor in popular superstition. The following story from Gervase of Tilbury exhibits him in one of his mildest and most beneficent appearances :

" Est in Anglia quoddam dæmonum genus quod suo idiomate Grant nominant, ad instar pulli equini anniculi, tibiis erectum, oculis scintillantibus. Istud dæmonum genus sæpissime comparet in plateis, in ipsius diei fervore, aut circa solis occiduum. Et quoties apparet futurum in urbe illa vel vico portendit incendium. Cum ergo, sequente die vel nocte, instat periculum, in plateis discursu facto canes provocat ad latrandum, et dum fugam simulat sequentes canes ad insequendum spe vana consequendi invitat. Hujusmodi illusio convicaneis de ignis custodia cautelam facit, et hic officiorum dæmonum genus, dum conspicientes terret, suo adventu munire ignorantes solet."—C. 62.

In Denmark an extraordinary custom prevailed of burying a live animal—a horse, a lamb, a pig, and even a child—at the commencement of a building. It is strange that a similar custom appears, from the Servian Ballads, to have prevailed among the Slavonians. A lamb was generally entombed in the foundation of a church ; a horse in that of the churchyard. This horse, the peasants say, appears again and goes round the churchyard on three legs; when he meets any one he displays his grinning teeth—and death accompanies him. He is therefore called the *Hælhest**, the death-horse; and it is usual for a person on recovering from a fit of sickness, to say—"I have given Death a bushel of oats." Keysler (Antiq. Sept. et Celt. p. 181) says; "In ducatu Slesvicensi ea superstitio etiamnum obtinet, ut Hel dicant mortem vel spectrum tempore pestis equo (qui tribus tantum pedibus incedit) inequitans mortalesque trucidans. Vico vel oppido fatali hoc contagio afflato vulgus ait Helam circumire *Der Hell geht umher.* Canes etiam tum ab ea inquietari indicant formula *Der Hell ist bey denen Hunden.*" This last circumstance reminds us of the classic Hecate, the rest of the sublime apparition of Death on his pale horse in the Apocalypse.

* Hæl was the Pluto of the ancient Scandinavians.

FAIRY LEGENDS.

THE FIR DARRIG.

Whene'er such wanderers I meete,
As from their night-sports they trudge home,
With counterfeiting voice I greete,
And call them on, with me to roame
Through woods, through lakes,
Through bogs, through brakes;
Or else, unseene, with them I go,
All in the nicke,
To play some tricke,
And frolicke it, with ho, ho, ho!

OLD SONG.

DIARMID BAWN, THE PIPER.

ONE stormy night Patrick Burke was seated in the chimney corner, smoking his pipe quite contentedly after his hard day's work; his two little boys were roasting potatoes in the ashes, while his rosy daughter held a splinter * to her mother, who, seated on a siesteen †, was mending a rent in Patrick's old coat; and Judy, the maid, was singing merrily to the sound of her wheel, that kept up a beautiful humming noise, just like the sweet drone of a bagpipe. Indeed they all seemed quite contented and happy; for the storm howled without, and they were warm and snug within, by the side of a blazing turf fire. "I was just thinking," said Patrick, taking the du-

* A splinter, or slip of bog-deal, which, being dipped in tallow, is used as a candle.

† Siesteen is a low block-like seat, made of straw bands firmly sewed or bound together.

deen from his mouth and giving it a rap on his thumb-nail to shake out the ashes—"I was just thinking how thankful we ought to be to have a snug bit of a cabin this pelting night over our heads, for in all my born days I never heard the like of it."

"And that's no lie for you, Pat," said his wife; "but, whisht! what noise is that I *hard?*" and she dropped her work upon her knees, and looked fearfully towards the door. "The *Vargin* herself defend us all!" cried Judy, at the same time rapidly making a pious sign on her forehead, "if 'tis not the banshee!"

"Hold your tongue, you fool," said Patrick, "it's only the old gate swinging in the wind;" and he had scarcely spoken, when the door was assailed by a violent knocking. Molly began to mumble her prayers, and Judy proceeded to mutter over the muster-roll of saints; the youngsters scampered off to hide themselves behind the settle-bed; the storm howled louder and more fiercely than ever, and the rapping was renewed with redoubled violence.

"Whisht, whisht!" said Patrick—"what a noise ye're all making about nothing at all. Judy a roon, can't you go and see who's at the door?" for, notwithstanding his assumed bravery, Pat

Burke preferred that the maid should open the door.

"Why, then, is it me you 're speaking to?" said Judy, in the tone of astonishment; "and is it cracked mad you are, Mister Burke; or is it, maybe, that you want me to be *rund* away with, and made a horse of, like my grandfather was?—the sorrow a step will I stir to open the door, if you were as great a man again as you are, Pat Burke."

"Bother you, then! and hold your tongue, and I 'll go myself." So saying, up got Patrick, and made the best of his way to the door. "Who 's there?" said he, and his voice trembled mightily all the while. "In the name of Saint Patrick, who 's there?" "'Tis I, Pat," answered a voice which he immediately knew to be the young squire's. In a moment the door was opened, and in walked a young man, with a gun in his hand, and a brace of dogs at his heels. "Your honour's honour is quite welcome, entirely," said Patrick; who was a very civil sort of a fellow, especially to his betters. "Your honour's honour is quite welcome; and if ye 'll be so condescending as to demean yourself by taking off your wet jacket, Molly can give ye a bran new blanket, and ye can sit forenent the fire while the clothes are drying."

"Thank you, Pat," said the squire, as he wrapt himself, like Mr. Weld, in the proffered blanket.*

"But what made you keep me so long at the door?"

"Why, then, your honour, 'twas all along of Judy, there, being so much afraid of the good people; and a good right she has, after what happened to her grandfather—the Lord rest his soul!"

"And what was that, Pat?" said the squire.

"Why, then, your honour must know that Judy had a grandfather; and he was *ould* Diarmid Bawn, the piper, as personable a looking man as any in the five parishes he was; and he could play the pipes so sweetly, and make them *spake* to such perfection, that it did one's heart good to hear him. We never had any one, for that matter, in this side of the country like him, before or since, except James Gandsey, that is own piper to Lord Headly—his honour's lordship is the real good gentleman—and 'tis Mr. Gandsey's music that is the pride of Killarney lakes. Well, as I was saying, Diarmid was Judy's grandfather, and he rented a small mountainy farm; and he was walking about the fields one moonlight night, quite melancholy-like in himself for want of the *Tobaccy;* because, why, the river was flooded, and he could not get

* See Weld's Killarney, 8vo ed. p. 228.

across to buy any, and Diarmid would rather go to bed without his supper than a whiff of the dudeen. Well, your honour, just as he came to the old fort in the far field, what should he see? —the Lord preserve us!—but a large army of the good people, 'coutered for all the world just like the dragoons! 'Are ye all ready?' said a little fellow at their head dressed out like a general. 'No;' said a little curmudgeon of a chap all dressed in red, from the crown of his cocked hat to the sole of his boot. 'No, general,' said he; 'if you don't get the Fir darrig a horse he must stay behind, and ye 'll lose the battle."

"'There 's Diarmid Bawn,' said the general, pointing to Judy's grandfather, your honour, 'make a horse of him.'

"So with that master Fir darrig comes up to Diarmid, who, you may be sure, was in a mighty great fright; but he determined, seeing there was no help for him, to put a bold face on the matter; and so he began to cross himself, and to say some blessed words, that nothing bad could stand before.

"'Is that what you 'd be after, you spalpeen?' said the little red imp, at the same time grinning a horrible grin; 'I 'm not the man to care a straw for either your words or your crossings.' So, without more to do, he gives poor Diarmid a rap with the flat side of his sword, and in a moment he was changed into a horse, with little Fir darrig stuck fast on his back.

" Away they all flew over the wide ocean, like so many wild geese, screaming and chattering all the time, till they came to Jamaica; and there they had a murdering fight with the good people of that country. Well, it was all very well with them, and they stuck to it manfully, and fought it ought fairly, 'till one of the Jamaica men made a cut with his sword under Diarmid's left eye, and then, sir, you see, poor Diarmid lost his temper entirely, and he dashed into the very middle of them, with Fir darrig mounted up on his back, and he threw out his heels, and he whisked his tail about, and wheeled and turned round and round at such a rate, that he soon made a fair clearance of them, horse, foot, and dragoons. At last, Diarmid's faction got the better, all through his means; and then they had such feasting and rejoicing, and gave Diarmid, who was the finest horse amongst them all, the best of every thing.

" 'Let every man take a hand of *Tobaccy* for Diarmid Bawn,' said the general; and so they did; and away they flew, for 'twas getting near morning, to the old fort back again, and there they vanished like the mist from the mountain.

" When Diarmid looked about the sun was rising, and he thought it was all a dream, till he

Poor Diarmid lost his temper entirely

saw a big rick of *Tobaccy* in the old fort, and felt the blood running from his left eye; for sure enough he was wounded in the battle, and would have been *kilt* entirely, if it wasn't for a gospel composed by father Murphy that hung about his neck ever since he had the scarlet fever; and for certain, it was enough to have given him another scarlet fever to have had the little red man all night on his back, whip and spur for the bare life. However, there was the *Tobaccy* heaped up in a great heap by his side; and he heard a voice, although he could see no one, telling him, 'That 'twas all his own, for his good behaviour in the battle; and that whenever Fir darrig would want a horse again he'd know where to find a clever beast, as he never rode a better than Diarmid Bawn.' That's what he said, sir."

"Thank you, Pat," said the squire; "it certainly is a wonderful story, and I am not surprised at Judy's alarm. But now, as the storm is over, and the moon shining brightly, I'll make the best of my way home." So saying, he disrobed himself of the blanket, put on his coat, and, whistling his dogs, set off across the mountain; while Patrick stood at the door, bawling after him, "May God and the blessed Virgin preserve your honour, and keep ye from the good people;

for 'twas of a moonlight night like this that Diarmid Bawn was made a horse of, for the Fir darrig to ride.

Fir Darrig, correctly written, *fear dearg*, means the red man, and is a member of the fairy tribe of Ireland, who bears a great resemblance to the Puck or Robin Goodfellow of Shakspeare's days. Like that merry goblin, his delight is in mischief and mockery; and numberless are the wild and whimsical stories in which he figures. Although the German Kobolds partake of the good-natured character of the people, yet the celebrated Hinzelman occasionally amused himself with playing tricks somewhat similar to those of master Fir darrig.

The red dress and strange flexibility of voice possessed by the Fir darrig form his peculiar characteristics; the latter is said, by Irish tale-tellers, to be as *Fuaim na dtonn*, the sound of the waves; and again it is compared to *Ceol na naingeal*, the music of angels; *Ceileabhar na nèan*, the warbling of birds, &c.; and the usual address to this fairy is, *Na dean fochmoid fùinn*, do not mock us. His entire dress, when he is seen, is invariably described as crimson; whereas, the fairies generally appear in *Hata dubh, culaigh ghlas, stocaigh bana, agus broga dearga*; a black hat, a green suit, white stockings, and red shoes.

The transformation of Diarmid into a horse is no uncommon one. Circe used to transmute people by hundreds. Queen Labe and Co. in the Arabian Nights were equally expert at metamorphoses; a horse, by-the-bye, was the very form that queen gave king Beder, who, however, had previously transformed her majesty into a mare. King Carpalus, too, in the old romance of Ogier le Dannoys, was condemned to spend three hundred years in the form of a horse, for the resistance he made to king Arthur in Fairy land.

Diarmid Bawn signifies white or fair Edward. "A Gospel," to which he owes his preservation in the fairy fight, is a text of scripture written in a particular manner, and which has been blessed by a priest. It is sewed in red cloth, and hung round the neck as a cure or preventive against various diseases, &c. Few Irish peasants will be found without "a gospel;" or, as in the vicinity of Holy Cross, a blessed string, a blessed stone, or a blessed bit of wood, about their persons, which they consider to be an infallible safeguard against evil. Indeed, the popular mind at the present moment is full as credulous in these matters as it was nearly two centuries since, when lord Broghill captured a "peckful of spells and charms" among the baggage, after defeating lord Muskerry.

TEIGUE OF THE LEE.

"I CAN'T stop in the house—I won't stop in it for all the money that is buried in the old castle of Carrigrohan. If ever there was such a thing in the world!—to be abused to my face night and day, and nobody to the fore doing it! and then, if I 'm angry, to be laughed at with a great roaring ho, ho, ho! I won't stay in the house after to-night, if there was not another place in the country to put my head under." This angry soliloquy was pronounced in the hall of the old manor-house of Carrigrohan by John Sheehan. John was a new servant; he had been only three days in the house, which had the character of being haunted, and in that short space of time he had been abused and laughed at, by a voice which sounded as if a man spoke with his head in a cask; nor could he discover who was the speaker, or from whence the voice came. "I 'll not stop here," said John; "and that ends the matter."

"Ho, ho, ho! be quiet, John Sheehan, or else worse will happen to you."

John instantly ran to the hall window, as the

words were evidently spoken by a person immediately outside, but no one was visible. He had scarcely placed his face at the pane of glass, when he heard another loud "Ho, ho, ho!" as if behind him in the hall; as quick as lightning he turned his head, but no living thing was to be seen.

"Ho, ho, ho, John!" shouted a voice that appeared to come from the lawn before the house; "do you think you 'll see Teigue?—oh, never! as long as you live! so leave alone looking after him, and mind your business; there 's plenty of company to dinner from Cork to be here to-day, and 'tis time you had the cloth laid."

"Lord bless us! there 's more of it!—I 'll never stay another day here," repeated John.

"Hold your tongue, and stay where you are quietly, and play no tricks on Mr. Pratt, as you did on Mr. Jervois about the spoons."

John Sheehan was confounded by this address from his invisible persecutor, but nevertheless he mustered courage enough to say—"Who are you?—come here, and let me see you, if you are a man;" but he received in reply only a laugh of unearthly derision, which was followed by a "Good bye—I 'll watch you at dinner, John!"

"Lord between us and harm! this beats all!—I 'll watch you at dinner!—maybe you will;—'tis the broad day-light, so 'tis no ghost; but this is a terrible place, and this is the last day I 'll stay in it. How does he know about the spoons?—if he tells it, I 'm a ruined man!—there was no living soul could tell it to him but Tim Barrett, and he 's far enough off in the wilds of Botany Bay now, so how could he know it—I can't tell for the world! But what 's that I see there at the corner of the wall!—'tis not a man!—oh, what a fool I am! 'tis only the old stump of a tree!—But this is a shocking place—I 'll never stop in it, for I 'll leave the house to-morrow; the very look of it is enough to frighten any one."

The mansion had certainly an air of desolation; it was situated in a lawn, which had nothing to break its uniform level, save a few tufts of narcissuses and a couple of old trees coeval with the building. The house stood at a short distance from the road, it was upwards of a century old, and Time was doing his work upon it; its walls were weather-stained in all colours, its roof showed various white patches, it had no look of comfort; all was dim and dingy without, and within there was an air of gloom, of departed and departing greatness, which harmonised well with the exterior. It required all the exuberance of youth and of gaiety to remove the impression, almost amounting to awe, with which you trod the huge square hall, paced along the gallery which surrounded the hall, or explored the long rambling passages below stairs. The ball-room, as the large drawing-room was called, and several other apartments were in a state of decay; the walls were stained with damp, and I remember well the sensation of awe which I felt creeping over me when, boy as I was, and full of boyish life, and wild and ardent spirits, I descended to the vaults; all without and within me became chilled beneath their dampness and gloom—their extent, too, terrified me; nor could the merriment of my two schoolfellows, whose father, a respectable clergyman, rented the dwelling for a time, dispel the feelings of a romantic imagination until I once again ascended to the upper regions.

John had pretty well recovered himself as the dinner-hour approached, and several guests arrived. They were all seated at table, and had begun to enjoy the excellent repast, when a voice was heard in the lawn.

"Ho, ho, ho, Mr. Pratt, won't you give poor Teigue some dinner? ho, ho, a fine company you have there, and plenty of every thing that's good; sure you won't forget poor Teigue?"

John dropped the glass he had in his hand.

"Who is that?" said Mr. Pratt's brother, an officer of the artillery.

"That is Teigue," said Mr. Pratt, laughing, "whom you must often have heard me mention."

"And pray, Mr. Pratt," inquired another gentleman, "who *is* Teigue?"

"That," he replied, "is more than I can tell. No one has ever been able to catch even a glimpse of him. I have been on the watch for a whole evening with three of my sons, yet, although his voice sometimes sounded almost in my ear, I could not see him. I fancied, indeed, that I saw a man in a white frieze jacket pass into the door from the garden to the lawn, but it could be only fancy, for I found the door locked, while the fellow, whoever he is, was laughing at our trouble. He visits us occasionally, and sometimes a long interval passes between his visits, as in the present case; it is now nearly two years since we heard that hollow voice outside the window. He has never done any injury that we know of, and once when he broke a plate, he brought one back exactly like it."

"It is very extraordinary," said several of the company.

"But," remarked a gentleman to young Mr. Pratt, "your father said he broke a plate; how did he get it without your seeing him?"

"When he asks for some dinner, we put it

outside the window and go away; whilst we watch he will not take it, but no sooner have we withdrawn than it is gone."

"How does he know that you are watching?"

"That 's more than I can tell, but he either knows or suspects. One day my brothers Robert and James with myself were in our back parlour, which has a window into the garden, when he came outside and said, 'Ho, ho, ho! master James, and Robert, and Henry, give poor Teigue a glass of whiskey.' James went out of the room, filled a glass with whiskey, vinegar, and salt, and brought it to him. 'Here, Teigue,' said he, 'come for it now.' 'Well, put it down, then, on the step outside the window.' This was done, and we stood looking at it. 'There, now, go away,' he shouted. We retired, but still watched it. 'Ho, ho! you are watching Teigue; go out of the room, now, or I won't take it.' We went outside the door and returned, the glass was gone, and a moment after we heard him roaring and cursing frightfully. He took away the glass, but the next day the glass was on the stone step under the window, and there were crums of bread in the inside, as if he had put it in his pocket; from that time he was not heard till to-day."

"Oh," said the colonel, "I 'll get a sight of him; you are not used to these things; an old soldier has the best chance, and as I shall finish my dinner with this wing, I 'll be ready for him when he speaks next.—Mr. Bell, will you take a glass of wine with me?"

"Ho, ho! Mr. Bell," shouted Teigue. "Ho, ho! Mr. Bell, you were a quaker long ago. Ho, ho! Mr. Bell, you 're a pretty boy;—a pretty quaker you were; and now you 're no quaker, nor any thing else:—ho, ho! Mr. Bell. And there 's Mr. Parkes: to be sure, Mr. Parkes looks mighty fine to-day, with his powdered head, and his grand silk stockings, and his bran new rakish-red waistcoat.—And there 's Mr. Cole,—did you ever see such a fellow? a pretty company you 've brought together, Mr. Pratt: kiln-dried quakers, butter-buying buckeens from Mallow-lane, and a drinking exciseman from the Coal-quay, to meet the great thundering artillery-general that is come out of the Indies, and is the biggest dust of them all."

"You scoundrel!" exclaimed the colonel: "I'll make you show yourself;" and snatching up his sword from a corner of the room, he sprang out of the window upon the lawn. In a moment a shout of laughter, so hollow, so unlike any human sound, made him stop, as well as Mr. Bell, who with a huge oak stick was close at the colonel's heels; others of the party followed on the lawn, and the remainder rose and went to the windows.

"Come on, colonel," said Mr. Bell; "let us catch this impudent rascal."

"Ho, ho! Mr. Bell, here I am—here 's Teigue—why don't you catch him?—Ho, ho! colonel Pratt, what a pretty soldier you are to draw your sword upon poor Teigue, that never did any body harm."

"Let us see your face, you scoundrel," said the colonel.

"Ho, ho, ho!—look at me—look at me: do you see the wind, colonel Pratt?—you 'll see Teigue as soon; so go in and finish your dinner."

"If you 're upon the earth I 'll find you, you villain!" said the colonel, whilst the same unearthly shout of derision seemed to come from behind an angle of the building. "He 's round that corner," said Mr. Bell—"run, run."

They followed the sound, which was continued at intervals along the garden wall, but could discover no human being; at last both stopped to draw breath, and in an instant, almost at their ears, sounded the shout.

"Ho, ho, ho! colonel Pratt, do you see Teigue now?—do you hear him?—Ho, ho, ho! you 're a fine colonel to follow the wind."

"Not that way, Mr. Bell—not that way; come here," said the colonel.

"Ho, ho, ho! what a fool you are; do you

think Teigue is going to show himself to you in the field, there? But, colonel, follow me if you can:—you a soldier!—ho, ho, ho!" The colonel was enraged—he followed the voice over hedge and ditch, alternately laughed at and taunted by the unseen object of his pursuit—(Mr. Bell, who was heavy, was soon thrown out), until at length, after being led a weary chase, he found himself at the top of the cliff, over that part of the river Lee which, from its great depth, and the blackness of its water, has received the name of Hell-hole. Here, on the edge of the cliff, stood the colonel out of breath, and mopping his forehead with his handkerchief, while the voice, which seemed close at his feet, exclaimed—"Now, colonel Pratt—now, if you're a soldier, here's a leap for you;—now look at Teigue—why don't you look at him? —Ho, ho, ho! Come along; you're warm, I'm sure, colonel Pratt, so come in and cool yourself; Teigue is going to have a swim!" The voice seemed as descending amongst the trailing ivy and brushwood which clothes this picturesque cliff nearly from top to bottom, yet it was impossible that any human being could have found footing. "Now, colonel, have you courage to take the leap?—Ho, ho, ho! what a pretty soldier you are. Good-bye—I'll see you again in ten minutes above, at the house—look at your watch, colonel:—there's a dive for you ;" and a heavy plunge into the water was heard. The colonel stood still, but no sound followed, and he walked slowly back to the house, not quite half a mile from the Crag."

"Well, did you see Teigue?" said his brother, whilst his nephews, scarcely able to smother their laughter, stood by.—"Give me some wine," said the colonel. "I never was led such a dance in my life; the fellow carried me all round and round, till he brought me to the edge of the cliff, and then down he went into Hell-hole, telling me he'd be here in ten minutes: 'tis more than that now, but he's not come."

"Ho, ho, ho! colonel, isn't he here?—Teigue never told a lie in his life: but, Mr. Pratt, give me a drink and my dinner, and then good night to you all, for I'm tired; and that's the colonel's doing." A plate of food was ordered; it was placed by John, with fear and trembling, on the lawn under the window. Every one kept on the watch, and the plate remained undisturbed for some time.

"Ah! Mr. Pratt, will you starve poor Teigue? Make every one go away from the windows, and master Henry out of the tree, and master Richard off the garden wall."

The eyes of the company were turned to the tree and the garden wall; the two boys' attention was occupied in getting down; the visitors were looking at them; and "Ho, ho, ho!—good luck to you, Mr. Pratt!—'tis a good dinner, and there's the plate, ladies and gentlemen—good-bye to you, colonel!—good-bye, Mr. Bell!—good-bye to you all"—brought their attention back, when they saw the empty plate lying on the grass; and Teigue's voice was heard no more for that evening. Many visits were afterwards paid by Teigue; but never was he seen, nor was any discovery ever made of his person or character.

The pranks of Teigue resemble those related by Gervase of Tilbury of the spirit called Follet, which he describes as inhabiting the houses of ignorant rustics, and whose exorcisms fail in banishing him. He says of the Folletos:

"Verba utique humano more audiuntur et effigies non comparent. De istis pleraque miracula memini me *in vita abbreviata et miraculis beatissimi Antonii reperisse.*"—Otia Imperalia, p. 897.

Their voices may be heard in human fashion, but their form is not visible. I remember to have read a great many marvels about them in the short life and miracles of the blessed Anthony.

The evening previous to sending this note to press, it was the writer's good fortune to meet major Percy

Pratt, son of the colonel (afterwards general) Pratt mentioned in the tale, who related to Sir William Beetham, and repeated to him, all the particulars of this strange story. Several respectable persons in the south of Ireland have favoured him with accounts of Teigue, but they are so nearly similar that it becomes unnecessary to give them. One of these accounts, however, received from Mr. Newenham de la Cour, contains some few circumstances which have been omitted in the foregoing relation:

"I never heard," writes Mr. de la Cour, "of a more familiar goblin than Teigue. His visit generally commenced with a civil salutation to the master of the house, which was quickly followed by an application for a glass of whiskey; but no human creature could be seen or found in the quarter from whence the voice proceeded. These visits were usually repeated once a week; sometimes, however, a month or more elapsed between them. If any friend came to dine or to stay at the house for a few days, Teigue was sure to be heard in the evening accosting them in a very courteous manner, inquiring after the different members of their family, and often mentioning domestic occurrences with a surprising intimacy. If a stranger happened to excel in music, this could not escape the penetration of Teigue, who seemed to be familiar with every person's acquirements and habits; and he invariably requested the musician to play or sing. A young lady from Youghall was once called on by Teigue to favour him with a tune: she sat down to the pianoforte all fear and trembling. When she had concluded, Teigue applauded her performance, and said, in return, he would treat her to a song to the best of his ability. He accordingly sung, with a most tremendous voice, 'My name is Teigue, and I lives in state;' a composition well known in the south of Ireland.

"Several cleverly concerted plans have been formed for the discovery of this strange being, yet they all failed of their object. Two different and contradictory opinions prevail respecting Teigue: some people report him to be a giant, others a dwarf; the former opinion is founded on the following circumstance:—Amongst the ingenious methods devised for deciding whether the voice might be that of a mortal man or a goblin was the plan of strewing carefully some fine ashes at twilight before the windows. That night Teigue was unusually noisy without; and the next morning early, when the place was inspected, the print of one foot only, of superhuman dimensions, was found. The notion of his being a dwarf rests on no less an authority than Teigue himself. He frequently styled himself Teigueen, or little Teigue; yet this diminutive may be nothing more than a pet name. But on one occasion, when some guests expressed their surprise that master Teigue had never been caught, this curious being replied, ''Tis to no use at all, gentlemen, you 're thinking of catching poor Teigueen, for he is no bigger than your thumb!' All those who have heard him speak agree in this, that the sound of his voice was not in the least like that of ordinary mortals; it resembled, they said, that hollow hoarse kind of voice emitted by a man speaking with his head (as a gallant English officer has described it) inclosed in an *empty* cask."

Connected with the belief of supernatural voices, a common superstitious notion may be worth mentioning here. It is popularly believed in Ireland, and possibly in other countries, that when a friend or relative dies a warning voice is heard, and the greater the space between the parties the more certain the sound. The following is an attempt at translating an Irish song founded on this idea, which is sung to a singularly wild and melancholy air:

A low sound of song from the distance I hear,
In the silence of night, breathing sad on my ear!
Whence comes it? I know not—unearthly the note,
And unearthly the tones through the air as they float;
Yet it sounds like the lay that my mother once sung,
As o'er her first-born in his cradle she hung.

Long parted from her, far away from her home,
'Mong people that speak not her language I roam:
Is it she that sends over the billowy sea
This low-breathing murmur of sadness to me!
What gives it the power thus to shake me with dread?
Does it say, that sad voice, that my mother is dead?

NED SHEEHY'S EXCUSE.

Ned Sheehy was servant-man to Richard Gumbleton, esq. of Mountbally, Gumbletonmore, in the north of the county of Cork; and a better servant than Ned was not to be found in that honest county, from Cape Clear to the Kilworth Mountains; for no body—no, not his worst enemy, could say a word against him, only that he was rather given to drinking, idling, lying, and loitering, especially the last, for send Ned of a five minute message at nine o'clock in the morning, and you were a lucky man if you saw him before dinner. If there happened to be a public-house in the way, or even a little out of it, Ned was sure to mark it as dead as a pointer; and knowing every body, and every body liking him, it is not to be wondered at he had so much to say and to hear, that the time slipped away as if the sun somehow or other had knocked two hours into one.

But when he came home, he never was short of an excuse; he had, for that matter, five hundred ready upon the tip of his tongue, so much so, that I doubt if even the very reverend doctor

Swift, for many years Dean of St. Patrick's, in Dublin, could match him in that particular, though his reverence had a pretty way of his own of writing things which brought him into very decent company. In fact, Ned would fret a saint, but then he was so good-humoured a fellow, and really so handy about a house, for, as he said himself, he was as good as a lady's-maid, that his master could not find it in his heart to part with him.

In your grand houses—not that I am saying that Richard Gumbleton, esquire, of Mountbally, Gumbletonmore, did not keep a good house, but a plain country gentleman, although he is second cousin to the last high-sheriff of the county, cannot have all the army of servants that the lord-lieutenant has in the castle of Dublin—I say, in your grand houses, you can have a servant for every kind of thing, but in Mountbally, Gumbletonmore, Ned was expected to please master and mistress; or, as counsellor Curran said,—by the same token the counsellor was a little dark man—one day that he dined there, on his way to the Clonmel assizes—Ned was minister for the home and foreign departments.

But to make a long story short, Ned Sheehy was a good butler, and a right good one too, and as for a groom, let him alone with a horse; he could dress it, or ride it, or shoe it, or physic it, or do any thing with it but make it speak—he was a second whisperer!—there was not his match in the barony, or the next one neither. A pack of hounds he could manage well, ay, and ride after them with the boldest man in the land. It was Ned who leaped the old bounds ditch at the turn of the boreen of the lands of Reenascreena, after the English captain pulled up on looking at it, and cried out it was "No go." Ned rode that day Brian Boro, Mr. Gumbleton's famous chesnut, and people call it Ned Sheehy's leap to this hour.

So, you see, it was hard to do without him; however, many a scolding he got, and although his master often said of an evening, "I'll turn off Ned," he always forgot to do so in the morning. These threats mended Ned not a bit; indeed he was mending the other way, like bad fish in hot weather.

One cold winter's day, about three o'clock in the afternoon, Mr. Gumbleton said to him,

"Ned," said he, "go take Modderaroo down to black Falvey, the horse-doctor, and bid him look at her knees, for Doctor Jenkinson, who rode her home last night, has hurt her somehow. I suppose he thought a parson's horse ought to go upon its knees; but, indeed, it was I was the fool to give her to him at all, for he sits twenty stone if he sits a pound, and knows no more of riding, particularly after his third bottle, than I do of preaching. Now mind and be back in an hour at furthest, for I want to have the plate cleaned up properly for dinner, as sir Augustus O'Toole, you know, is to dine here to-day.—Don't loiter for your life."

"Is it I, sir?" says Ned. "Well, that beats any thing; as if I'd stop out a minute!" So mounting Modderaroo, off he set.

Four, five, six o'clock came, and so did sir Augustus and lady O'Toole, and the four misses O'Toole, and Mr. O'Toole, and Mr. Edward O'Toole, and Mr. James O'Toole, which were all the young O'Tooles that were at home, but no Ned Sheehy appeared to clean the plate, or to lay the table-cloth, or even to put dinner on. It is needless to say how Mr. and Mrs. Dick Gumbleton fretted and fumed, but it was all to no use. They did their best, however, only it was a disgrace to see long Jem the stable-boy, and Bill the gossoon that used to go of errands, waiting, without any body to direct them, when there was a real baronet and his lady at table, for sir Augustus was none of your knights. But a good bottle of claret makes up for much, and it was not one only they had that night. However it is not to be concealed that Mr. Dick Gumbleton went to bed very cross, and he awoke still crosser.

He heard that Ned had not made his appearance for the whole night, so he dressed himself in a great fret, and taking his horsewhip in his hand he said,

"There is no further use in tolerating this scoundrel; I'll go look for him, and if I find him, I'll cut the soul out of his vagabond body! I will by —"

"Don't swear, Dick dear," said Mrs. Gumbleton (for she was always a mild woman, being daughter of fighting Tom Crofts, who shot a couple of gentlemen, friends of his, in the cool of the evening, after the Mallow races, one after the other), "don't swear, Dick, dear," said she, "but do, my dear, oblige me by cutting the flesh off his bones, for he richly deserves it. I was quite ashamed of lady O'Toole, yesterday, I was, 'pon honour."

Out sallied Mr. Gumbleton; and he had not far to walk; for not more than two hundred yards from the house, he found Ned lying fast asleep under a ditch *, and Modderaroo standing by him, poor beast, shaking every limb. The loud snoring of Ned, who was lying with his head upon a stone as easy and as comfortable as if it had been a bed of down or a hop-bag, drew him to the spot, and

* Ditch, a hedge.

Mr. Gumbleton at once perceived, from the disarray of Ned's face and person, that he had been engaged in some perilous adventure during the night. Ned appeared not to have descended in the most regular manner, for one of his shoes remained sticking in the stirrups, and his hat, having rolled down a little slope, was imbedded in green mud. Mr. Gumbleton, however, did not give himself much trouble to make a curious survey, but with a vigorous application of his thong soon banished sleep from the eyes of Ned Sheehy.

"Ned," thundered his master in great indignation; and on this occasion it was not a word and blow, for with that one word came half a dozen. "Get up, you scoundrel," said he.

Ned roared lustily, and no wonder, for his master's hand was not one of the lightest; and he cried out, between sleeping and waking—"O, sir! —don't be angry, sir!—don't be angry, and I'll roast you easier—easy as a lamb!"

"Roast me easier, you vagabond!" said Mr. Gumbleton; "what do you mean?—I'll roast you, my lad. Where were you all night?—Modderaroo will never get over it.—Pack out of my service, you worthless villain, this moment; and, indeed, you may give God thanks that I don't get you transported."

"Thank God, master, dear," said Ned, who

was now perfectly awakened—" it 's yourself anyhow. There never was a gentleman in the whole county ever did so good a turn to a poor man as your honour has been after doing to me: the Lord reward you for that same. Oh! but strike me again, and let me feel that it is yourself, master, dear;—may whiskey be my poison—"

" It will be your poison, you good-for-nothing scoundrel," said Mr. Gumbleton.

" Well, then, *may* whiskey be my poison," said Ned, " if 'twas not I was—God help me!—in the blackest of misfortunes, and they were before me, whichever way I turned 'twas no matter. Your honour sent me last night, sure enough, with Modderaroo to mister Falvey's—I don't deny it —why should I? for reason enough I have to remember what happened."

" Ned, my man," said Mr. Gumbleton, " I 'll listen to none of your excuses: just take the mare into the stable and yourself off, for I vow to —"

" Begging your honour's pardon," said Ned, earnestly, " for interrupting your honour; but, master, master! make no vows—they are bad things: I never made but one in all my life, which was to drink nothing at all for a year and a day, and 'tis myself repinted of it for the clean twelvemonth after. But if your honour would only listen to reason; I 'll just take in the poor baste, and if your honour don't pardon me this one time may I never see another day's luck or grace."

"I know you, Ned," said Mr. Gumbleton. "Whatever your luck has been, you never had any grace to lose: but I don't intend discussing the matter with you. Take in the mare, sir."

Ned obeyed, and his master saw him to the stables. Here he reiterated his commands to quit, and Ned Sheehy's excuse for himself began. That it was heard uninterruptedly is more than I can affirm; but as interruptions, like explanations, spoil a story, we must let Ned tell it his own way.

"No wonder your honour," said he, "should be a bit angry—grand company coming to the house and all, and no regular serving-man to wait, only long Jem; so I don't blame your honour the least for being fretted like; but when all 's heard, you will see that no poor man is more to be pitied for last night than myself. Fin Mac Coul never went through more in his born days than I did, though he was a great *joint* *, and I only a man.

"I had not rode half a mile from the house, when it came on, as your honour must have perceived clearly, mighty dark all of a sudden, for

* Giant.

all the world, as if the sun had tumbled down plump out of the fine clear blue sky. It was not so late, being only four o'clock at the most, but it was as black as your honour's hat. Well, I didn't care much, seeing I knew the road as well as I knew the way to my mouth, whether I saw it or not, and I put the mare into a smart canter; but just as I turned down by the corner of Terence Leahy's field—sure your honour ought to know the place well—just at the very spot the fox was killed when your honour came in first out of a whole field of a hundred and fifty gentlemen, and may be more, all of them brave riders."

(Mr. Gumbleton smiled.)

"Just then, there, I heard the low cry of the good people wafting upon the wind. How early you are at your work, my little fellows, says I to myself; and, dark as it was, having no wish for such company, I thought it best to get out of their way; so I turned the horse a little up to the left, thinking to get down by the boreen, that is that way, and so round to Falvey's, but there I heard the voice plainer and plainer close behind, and I could hear these words:

'Ned! Ned!
By my cap so red!
You 're as good, Ned,
As a man that is dead.'

A clean pair of spurs is all that 's for it now, said I; so off I set as hard as I could lick, and in my hurry knew no more where I was going than I do the road to the hill of Tara. Away I galloped on for some time, until I came to the noise of a stream, roaring away by itself in the darkness. What river is this? said I to myself—for there was nobody else to ask—I thought, says I, I knew every inch of ground, and of water too, within twenty miles, and never the river surely is there in this direction. So I stopped to look about; but I might have spared myself that trouble, for I could not see as much as my hand. I didn't know what to do; but I thought in myself, it 's a queer river, surely, if somebody does not live near it; and I shouted out, as loud as I could, Murder! murder!—fire!—robbery!—any thing that would be natural in such a place—but not a sound did I hear except my own voice echoed back to me, like a hundred packs of hounds in full cry, above and below, right and left. This didn't do at all; so I dismounted, and guided myself along the stream, directed by the noise of the water, as cautious as if I was treading upon eggs, holding poor Modderaroo by the bridle, who shook, the poor brute, all over in a tremble, like my old grandmother, rest her soul, anyhow! in the ague. Well, sir, the heart was sinking in me, and I was giving myself up, when, as good luck would have it, I saw a light. 'Maybe,' said I, 'my good fellow, you are only a jacky lanthorn, and want to bog me and Modderaroo.' But I looked at the light hard, and I thought it was too *study* (steady) for a jacky lanthorn. 'I 'll try you,' says I—'so here goes;' and walking as quick as a thief, I came towards it, being very near plumping into the river once or twice, and being stuck up to my middle, as your honour may perceive cleanly the marks of, two or three times in the *slob**. At last I made the light out, and it coming from a bit of a house by the road side; so I went to the door, and gave three kicks at it, as strong as I could.

" 'Open the door for Ned Sheehy,' said a voice inside. Now, besides that I could not, for the life of me, make out how any one inside should know me before I spoke a word at all, I did not like the sound of that voice, 'twas so hoarse and so hollow, just like a dead man's!—so I said nothing immediately. The same voice spoke again, and said, 'Why don't you open the door to Ned Sheehy?' 'How pat my name is to you,' said I, without speaking out, 'on tip of your tongue, like butter;' and I was between two minds about staying or going, when what should the door do but open,

* Or *slaib*; mire on the sea strand or river's bank.—O'Brien.

and out came a man holding a candle in his hand, and he had upon him a face as white as a sheet.

"'Why, then, Ned Sheehy,' says he, 'how grand you 're grown, that you won't come in and see a friend, as you 're passing by.'

"'Pray, sir,' says I, looking at him—though that face of his was enough to dumbfounder any honest man like myself—'Pray, sir,' says I, 'may I make so bold as to ask if you are not Jack Myers that was drowned seven years ago, next Martinmass, in the ford of Ah-na-fourish?'

"'Suppose I was,' says he; 'has not a man a right to be drowned in the ford facing his own cabin-door any day of the week that he likes, from Sunday morning to Saturday night?'

"'I 'm not denying that same, Mr. Myers, sir,' says I, 'if 'tis yourself is to the fore speaking to me.'

"'Well,' says he, 'no more words about that matter now; sure you and I, Ned, were friends of old; come in, and take a glass; and here 's a good fire before you, and nobody shall hurt or harm you, and I to the fore, and myself able to do it.'

"Now, your honour, though 'twas much to drink with a man that was drowned seven years before, in the ford of Ah-na-fourish, facing his own door, yet the glass was hard to be withstood

—to say nothing of the fire that was blazing within—for the night was mortal cold. So tying Modderaroo to the hasp of the door—if I don't love the creature as I love my own life—I went in with Jack Myers.

"Civil enough he was—I'll never say otherwise to my dying hour—for he handed me a stool by the fire, and bid me sit down and make myself comfortable. But his face, as I said before, was as white as the snow on the hills, and his two eyes fell dead on me, like the eyes of a cod without any life in them. Just as I was going to put the glass to my lips, a voice—'twas the same that I heard bidding the door be opened—spoke out of a cupboard that was convenient to the left hand side of the chimney, and said, 'Have you any news for me, Ned Sheehy?'

"'The never a word, sir,' says I, making answer before I tasted the whiskey, all out of civility; and to speak the truth, never the least could I remember at that moment of what had happened to me, or how I got there; for I was quite bothered with the fright.

"'Have you no news,' says the voice, 'Ned, to tell me, from Mountbally Gumbletonmore; or from the Mill; or about Moll Trantum that was married last week to Bryan Oge, and you at the wedding?'

"'No, sir,' says I, 'never the word.'

"'What brought you in here, Ned, then?' says the voice. I could say nothing; for whatever other people might do, I never could frame an excuse; and I was loth to say it was on account of the glass and the fire, for that would be to speak the truth.

"'Turn the scoundrel out,' says the voice; and at the sound of it, who would I see but Jack Myers making over to me with a lump of a stick in his hand, and it clenched on the stick so wicked. For certain, I did not stop to feel the weight of the blow; so, dropping the glass, and it full of the stuff too, I bolted out of the door, and never rested from running away, for as good I believe as twenty miles, till I found myself in a big wood.

"'The Lord preserve me! what will become of me, now!' says I. 'Oh, Ned Sheehy!' says I, speaking to myself, 'my man, you 're in a pretty hobble; and to leave poor Modderaroo after you!' But the words were not well out of my mouth, when I heard the dismallest ullagoane in the world, enough to break any one's heart that was not broke before, with the grief entirely; and it was not long 'till I could plainly see four men coming towards me, with a great black coffin on their shoulders. 'I'd better get up in a tree,' says I, 'for they say 'tis not lucky to meet a corpse: I'm in the way of misfortune to-night if ever man was.'

"I could not help wondering how a *berrin* * should come there in the lone wood at that time of night, seeing it could not be far from the dead hour. But it was little good for me thinking, for they soon came under the very tree I was roosting in, and down they put the coffin, and began to make a fine fire under me. I'll be smothered alive now, thinks I, and that will be the end of me; but I was afraid to stir for the life, or to speak out to bid them just make their fire under some other tree, if it would be all the same thing to them. Presently they opened the coffin, and out they dragged as fine looking a man as you'd meet with in a day's walk.

"'Where's the spit?' says one.

"'Here 'tis,' says another, handing it over; and for certain they spitted him, and began to turn him before the fire.

"If they are not going to eat him, thinks I, like the *Hannibals* father Quinlan told us about in his *sarmint* last Sunday.

* Funeral.

"I'm not here at all, Sir," says I

Published Dec. 1st 18[illegible] by [illegible] Murray London

"'Who'll turn the spit while we go for the other ingredients?' says one of them that brought the coffin, and a big ugly-looking blackguard he was.

"'Who'd turn the spit but Ned Sheehy?' says another.

"Burn you! thinks I, how should you know that I was here so handy to you up in the tree?

"'Come down, Ned Sheehy, and turn the spit,' says he.

"'I'm not here at all, sir,' says I, putting my hand over my face that he may not see me.

"'That won't do for you, my man,' says he; 'you'd better come down, or maybe I'd make you.'

"'I'm coming, sir,' says I, for 'tis always right to make a virtue of necessity. So down I came, and there they left me turning the spit in the middle of the wide wood.

"'Don't scorch me, Ned Sheehy, you vagabond,' says the man on the spit.

"'And my lord, sir, and ar'n't you dead, sir,' says I, 'and your honour taken out of the coffin and all?'

"'I ar'n't,' says he.

"'But surely you are, sir,' says I, 'for 'tis to no use now for me denying that I saw your honour, and I up in the tree.'

"'I ar'n't,' says he again, speaking quite short and snappish.

"So I said no more until presently he called out to me to turn him easy, or that may be 'twould be the worse turn for myself.

"'Will that do, sir?' says I, turning him as easy as I could.

"'That 's too easy,' says he; so I turned him faster.

"'That 's too fast,' says he; so finding that turn him which way I would, I could not please him, I got into a bit of a fret at last, and desired him to turn himself, for a grumbling spalpeen as he was, if he liked it better.

"Away I ran, and away he came hopping, spit and all after me, and he but half roasted. 'Murder!' says I, shouting out; 'I'm done for at long last—now or never!'—when all of a sudden, and 'twas really wonderful, not knowing where I was rightly, I found myself at the door of the very little cabin by the roadside that I had bolted out of from Jack Myers; and there was Modderaroo standing hard by.

"'Open the door for Ned Sheehy,' says the voice, for 'twas shut against me, and the door flew open in an instant. In I ran, without stop or stay, thinking it better to be beat by Jack Myers, he being an old friend of mine, than to be spitted like a Michaelmas goose by a man that I knew nothing about, either of him or his family, one or the other.

"'Have you any news for me?' says the voice, putting just the same question to me that it did before.

"'Yes, sir,' says I, 'and plenty.' So I mentioned all that had happened to me in the big wood, and how I got up in the tree, and how I was made come down again, and put to turning the spit, roasting the gentleman, and how I could not please him, turn him fast or easy, although I tried my best, and how he ran after me at last, spit and all.

"'If you had told me this before, you would not have been turned out in the cold,' said the voice.

"'And how could I tell it to you, sir,' says I, 'before it happened?'

"'No matter,' says he, 'you may sleep now till morning on that bundle of hay in the corner there, and only I was your friend, you'd have been *kilt* entirely.' So down I lay, but I was dreaming, dreaming all the rest of the night, and when you, master dear, woke me with that blessed blow, I thought 'twas the man on the spit had hold of me, and could hardly believe my eyes when I found myself in your honour's presence, and poor

Modderaroo safe and sound by my side; but how I came there is more than I can say, if 'twas not Jack Myers, although he did make the offer to strike me, or some one among the good people befriended me."

"It is all a drunken dream, you scoundrel," said Mr. Gumbleton; "have I not had fifty such execuses from you?"

"But never one, your honour, that really happened before," said Ned, with unblushing front. "Howsomever, since your honour fancies 'tis drinking I was, I'd rather never drink again to the world's end, than lose so good a master as yourself, and if I'm forgiven this once, and get another trial ——"

"Well," said Mr. Gumbleton, "you may, for this once, go into Mountbally Gumbletonmore again; let me see that you keep your promise as to not drinking, or mind the consequences; and above all, let me hear no more of the good people, for I don't believe a single word about them, whatever I may do of bad ones."

So saying, Mr. Gumbleton turned on his heel, and Ned's countenance relaxed into its usual expression.

"Now I would not be after saying about the good people what the master said last," exclaimed Peggy, the maid, who was within hearing, and who, by the way, had an eye after Ned: "I would not be after saying such a thing; the good people, maybe, will make him feel the *differ* (difference) to his cost."

Nor was Peggy wrong, for, whether Ned Sheehy dreamt of the Fir Darrig or not, within a fortnight after, two of Mr. Gumbleton's cows, the best milkers in the parish, ran dry, and before the week was out Modderaroo was lying dead in the stone quarry.

The name, and some of the situations in the foregoing tale are taken from Mr. Lynch's manuscript collection of Killarney legends, which has been most obligingly forwarded by him to the compiler of this volume. Several versions of this whimsical adventure are current in Ireland: one, which was noted down many years since, from the writer's nurse, is given as a proof how faithfully the main incidents in these tales are orally circulated and preserved. The heroine is Joan Coleman of Kinsale, who, after being driven out from an enchanted house, for having no story to tell, when called upon by an invisible speaker to do so, finds herself in a dark wood. Here she discovers a very old man, with a long beard, roasting another man as old as himself on a spit before a great fire.

"When the old man, who was turning the spit, saw Joan, he welcomed her, and expressed his joy at seeing his gossip's daughter, Joan Coleman of Kinsale. Joan was much frightened; but he welcomed her so kindly, and told her to sit down to the fire in so friendly a manner, that she was somewhat assured, and complied with the invitation. He then handed her the spit to turn, and gave her the strictest charge not to allow a brown or a burned spot on the old man who was roasting until he came back; and with these directions left her.

"It happened to be rather a windy night, and Joan had not turned the spit long before a spark flew into the beard of the roasting old man, and the wind blowing that way it was speedily on fire. Joan, when she saw what had happened, was much troubled, and ran away as fast as possible. When the old fellow felt his beard on fire, he called out to Joan, in a great passion, to come back, and not to allow him to be burned up to a cinder. Joan only ran the faster; and he, without ever getting off the spit, raced after her, with his beard all in flames, to know why, after the orders she had received, he was treated in that manner. Joan rushed into a house, which happened to be the very same that she had been turned out of for want of a story to tell. When she went in, Joan Coleman was welcomed by the same voice which had directed her to be turned out. She was desired to come to the fire, and pitied much, and a bed was ordered to be made for her. After she had lain down for some time, the voice asked her if she had now a story to tell? Joan answered that she had; having 'a fright in her heart,' from what had happened to her since she left, and without more words related her adventure. 'Very well,' said the voice, 'if you had told the same story when you were asked before, you would have had your comfortable lodging and your good night's rest by this time. I am sorry, Joan, that I was obliged to turn you out, that you might have something to tell me, for *Father Red Cap* never gives a bed without being paid for it by a story.' When Joan awoke next day at the crowing of the cock, she found herself lying on a little bank of rushes and green moss, with her bundle under her head for a pillow."

The Irish *Fir darrig* is doubtless the same as the Scottish *Red Cap;* and a writer in the Quarterly Review (No. XLIV. p. 358), tracing national analogies, says, that this fairy is the *Robin Hood* of England, and the Saxon spirit *Hudkin* or *Hodeken,* so called from the hoodakin or little hood which he wore.

Ned Sheehy, in his power over horses, is said to be a second Whisperer. To the English reader this may appear obscure, but it will be well understood in the south of Ireland. The reverend Horatio Townsend, in his valuable Statistical Survey of Cork, gives so remarkable an account of the Whisperer that the length of the extract will doubtless be pardoned.

"Among the curiosities of this district" (Newmarket) "may be properly included a very extraordinary power displayed by one of its natives, in controlling and subduing the refractory disposition of horses. What I am about to relate will appear almost incredible, and is certainly very hard to be accounted for; but there is not the least doubt of its truth. Many of the most respectable inhabitants have been witnesses of his performances, some of which came within my own knowledge.

"He was an awkward, ignorant rustic of the lowest class, of the name of Sullivan, but better known by the appellation of the Whisperer—his occupation, horse-breaking. The nickname he acquired from a vulgar notion of his being able to communicate to the animal what he wished by means of a whisper, and the singularity of his method seemed in some degree to justify the attribute. In his own neighbourhood, the notoriety of the fact made it appear less remarkable, but I doubt if any instance of similar subjugating talent is to be found on record. As far as the sphere of his control extended, the boast of *veni, vidi, vici*, was more justly claimed by Sullivan than by Cæsar himself. How his art was acquired, or in what it consisted, is likely to remain for ever unknown, as he has lately" (about 1810) "left the world without divulging it. His son, who follows the same trade, possesses but a small portion of the art, having either never learned the true secret, or being incapable of putting it in practice. The wonder of his skill consisted in the celerity of the operation, which was performed in privacy, and without any apparent means of coercion. Every description of horse, or even mule, whether previously broke or unhandled, whatever their peculiar vices or ill habits might have been, submitted without show of resistance to the magical influence of his art, and in the short space of half an hour became gentle and tractable. The effect, though instantaneously produced, was generally durable. Though more submissive to him than to others, they seemed to have acquired a docility unknown before. When sent for to tame a vicious beast, for which he was paid more or less, according to distance, generally two or three guineas, he directed the stable in which he and the object of the experiment were placed to be shut, with orders not to open the door until a signal given. After a tête-a-tête of about half an hour, during which little or no bustle was heard, the signal was made, and upon opening the door the horse appeared lying down, and the man by his side, playing familiarly with him, like a child with a puppy-dog. From that time he was found perfectly willing to submit to any discipline, however repugnant to his nature before.

"I once," continues Mr. Townsend, "saw his skill tried on a horse which could never before be brought to stand for a smith to shoe him. The day after Sullivan's half-hour lecture I went, not without some incredulity, to the smith's shop, with many other curious spectators, where we were eye-witnesses of the complete success of his art. This, too, had been a troop horse, and it was supposed, not without reason, that, after regimental discipline had failed, no other would be found availing. I observed that the animal appeared terrified whenever Sullivan either spoke or looked at him; how that extraordinary ascendancy could have been obtained it is difficult to conjecture. In common cases this mysterious preparation was unnecessary. He seemed to possess an instinctive power of inspiring awe, the result, perhaps, of natural intrepidity, in which I believe a great part of his art consisted, though the circumstance of the tête-à-tête shows that, upon particular occasions, something more must have been added to it. A faculty like this would, in other hands, have made a fortune, and I understand that great offers have been made to him for the exercise of his art abroad. But hunting was his passion. He lived at home in the style most agreeable to his disposition, and nothing could induce him to quit Duhallow and the fox-hounds."

THE LUCKY GUEST.

THE kitchen of some country houses in Ireland presents in no ways a bad modern translation of the ancient feudal hall. Traces of clanship still linger round its hearth in the numerous dependants on "the master's" bounty. Nurses, foster-brothers, and other hangers on, are there as matter of right, while the strolling piper, full of mirth and music, the benighted traveller, even the passing beggar, are received with a hearty welcome, and each contributes planxty, song, or superstitious tale, towards the evening's amusement.

An assembly, such as has been described, had collected round the kitchen fire of Ballyrahen-house, at the foot of the Galtee mountains, when, as is ever the case, one tale of wonder called forth another; and with the advance of the evening each succeeding story was received with deeper and deeper attention. The history of Cough na Looba's dance with the black friar at Rahill, and the fearful tradition of *Coum an 'ir morriv* (the dead man's hollow), were listened to in breathless silence. A pause followed the last relation, and all eyes rested on the narrator, an old nurse who occupied the post of honour, that next the fireside. She was seated in that peculiar position which the Irish name "*Currigguib,*" a position generally assumed by a veteran and determined story-teller. Her haunches resting upon the ground, and her feet bundled under the body; her arms folded across and supported by her knees, and the outstretched chin of her hooded head pressing on the upper arm; which compact arrangement nearly reduced the whole figure into a perfect triangle.

Unmoved by the general gaze, Bridget Doyle made no change of attitude, while she gravely asserted the truth of the marvellous tale concerning the Dead Man's Hollow; her strongly marked countenance at the time receiving what painters term a fine chiaro-scuro effect from the fire-light.

"I have told you," she said, "what happened to my own people, the Butlers and the Doyles, in the old times; but here is little Ellen Connell from the county Cork, who can speak to what happened under her own father and mother's roof —the Lord be good to them!"

Ellen was a young and blooming girl of about sixteen, who was employed in the dairy at Ballyrahen. She was the picture of health and rustic beauty; and at this hint from nurse Doyle, a deep blush mantled over her countenance; yet although "unaccustomed to public speaking," she, without further hesitation or excuse, proceeded as follows:

"It was one May eve, about thirteen years ago, and that is, as every body knows, the airiest day in all the twelve months. It is the day above all other," said Ellen, with her large dark eyes cast down on the ground, and drawing a deep sigh, "when the young boys and the young girls go looking after the *Drutheen,* to learn from it rightly the name of their sweethearts.

"My father, and my mother, and my two brothers, with two or three of the neighbours, were sitting round the turf fire, and were talking of one thing or another. My mother was hushoing my little sister, striving to quieten her, for she was cutting her teeth at the time, and was mighty uneasy through the means of them. The day, which was threatening all along, now that it was coming on to dusk, began to rain, and the rain increased and fell faster and faster, as if it was pouring through a sieve out of the wide heavens; and when the rain stopped for a bit there was a wind which kept up such a whistling and racket, that you would have thought the sky and the earth were coming together. It blew and it blew as if it had a mind to blow the roof off the cabin, and that would not have been very hard for it to do, as the thatch was quite loose in two or three places. Then the rain began again, and you could hear it spitting and hissing in the fire, as it came down through the big *chimbley*.

"'God bless us,' says my mother, 'but 'tis a dreadful night to be at sea,' says she, 'and God be praised that we have a roof, bad as it is, to shelter us.'

"I don't, to be sure, recollect all this, mistress Doyle, but only as my brothers told it to me, and other people, and often have I heard it; for I was so little then, that they say I could just go under the table without tipping my head. Any-way, it was in the very height of the pelting and whistling that we heard something speak outside the door. My father and all of us listened, but there was no more noise at that time. We waited a little longer, and then we plainly heard a sound like an old man's voice, asking to be let in, but mighty feebly and weak. Tim bounced up, with-out a word, to ask us whether we'd like to let the old man, or whoever he was, in—having al-ways a heart as soft as a mealy potatoe before the voice of sorrow. When Tim pulled back the bolt

All the eyes of our body were stuck upon him

Published [illegible]

that did the door, in marched a little bit of a shrivelled, weather-beaten creature, about two feet and a half high.

"We were all watching to see who'd come in, for there was a wall between us and the door; but when the sound of the undoing of the bolt stopped, we heard Tim give a sort of a screech, and instantly he bolted in to us. He had hardly time to say a word, or we either, when the little gentleman shuffled in after him, without a God save all here, or by your leave, or any other sort of thing that any decent body might say. We all, of one accord, scrambled over to the furthest end of the room, where we were, old and young, every one trying who'd get nearest the wall, and farthest from him. All the eyes of our body were stuck upon him, but he didn't mind us no more than that frying-pan there does now. He walked over to the fire, and squatting himself down like a frog, took the pipe that my father dropped from his mouth in the hurry, put it into his own, and then began to smoke so hearty, that he soon filled the room of it.

"We had plenty of time to observe him, and my brothers say that he wore a sugar-loaf hat that was as red as blood: he had a face as yellow as a kite's claw, and as long as to-day and to-morrow put together, with a mouth all screwed and puckered up like a washer-woman's hand, little blue eyes, and rather a highish nose; his hair was quite grey and lengthy, appearing under his hat, and flowing over the cape of a long scarlet coat which almost trailed the ground behind him, and the ends of which he took up and planked on his knees to dry, as he sat facing the fire. He had smart corduroy breeches, and woollen stockings drawn up over the knees, so as to hide the knee-buckles, if he had the pride to have them; but, at any rate, if he hadn't them in his knees he had them in his shoes, out before his spindle legs. When we came to ourselves a little we thought to escape from the room, but no one would go first, nor no one would stay last; so we huddled ourselves together and made a dart out of the room. My little gentleman never minded any thing of the scrambling, nor hardly stirred himself, sitting quite at his ease before the fire. The neighbours, the very instant minute they got to the door, although it still continued pelting rain, cut gutter as if Oliver Cromwell himself was at their heels; and no blame to them for that, anyhow. It was my father, and my mother, and my brothers, and myself, a little hop-of-my-thumb midge as I was then, that were left to see what would come out of this strange visit; so we all went quietly to the *labbig* *, scarcely daring to throw an eye at him as we passed the door. Never the wink of sleep could they sleep that live-long night, though, to be sure, I slept like a top, not knowing better, while they were talking and thinking of the little man.

" When they got up in the morning every thing was as quiet and as tidy about the place as if nothing had happened, for all that the chairs and stools were tumbled here, there, and everywhere, when we saw the lad enter. Now, indeed, I forget whether he came next night or not, but, anyway, that was the first time we ever laid eye upon him. This I know for certain, that, about a month after that, he came regularly every night, and used to give us a signal to be on the move, for 'twas plain he did not like to be observed. This sign was always made about eleven o'clock; and then, if we'd look towards the door, there was a little hairy arm thrust in through the key-hole, which would not have been big enough, only there was a fresh hole made near the first one, and the bit of stick between them had been broken away, and so 'twas just fitting for the little arm.

* *Labbig*—bed, from Leaba.—Vide O'BRIEN and O'REILLY.

"The Fir darrig continued his visits, never missing a night, as long as we attended to the signal; smoking always out of the pipe he made his own of, and warming himself till day dawned before the fire, and then going no one living knows where: but there was not the least mark of him to be found in the morning; and 'tis as true, nurse Doyle, and honest people, as you are all here sitting before me and by the side of me, that the family continued thriving, and my father and brothers rising in the world while ever he came to us. When we observed this, we used always look for the very moment to see when the arm would come, and then we'd instantly fly off with ourselves to our rest. But before we found the luck, we used sometimes sit still and not mind the arm, especially when a neighbour would be with my father, or that two or three or four of them would have a drop among them, and then they did not care for all the arms, hairy or not, that ever were seen. No one, however, dared to speak to it or of it insolently, except, indeed, one night that Davy Kennane—but he was drunk—walked over and hit it a rap on the back of the wrist: the hand was snatched off like lightning; but every one knows that Davy did not live a month after this happened, though he was only about ten days sick. The like of such tricks are ticklish things to do.

"As sure as the red man would put in his arm for a sign through the hole in the door, and that we did not go and open it to him, so sure some mishap befel the cattle: the cows were elf-stoned, or overlooked, or something or another went wrong with them. One night my brother Dan refused to go at the signal, and the next day, as he was cutting turf in Crogh-na-drimina bog, within a mile and a half of the house, a stone was thrown at him, which broke fairly, with the force, into two halves. Now, if that had happened to hit him, he'd be at this hour as dead as my great great-grandfather. It came whack-slap against the spade he had in his hand, and split at once in two pieces. He took them up and fitted them together, and they made a perfect heart. Some way or the other he lost it since, but he still has the one which was shot at the spotted milch cow, before the little man came near us. Many and many a time I saw that same; 'tis just the shape of the ace of hearts on the cards, only it is of a dark-red colour, and polished up like the grate that is in the grand parlour within. When this did not kill the cow on the spot, she swelled up; but if you took and put the elf-stone under her udder, and milked her upon it to the last stroking, and then made her drink the milk, it would cure her, and she would thrive with you ever after.

"But, as I said, we were getting on well enough as long as we minded the door and watched for the hairy arm, which we did sharp enough when we found it was bringing luck to us, and we were now as glad to see the little red gentleman, and as ready to open the door to him, as we used to dread his coming at first and be frightened of him. But at long last we throve so well that the landlord—God forgive him—took notice of us, and envied us, and asked my father how he came by the penny he had, and wanted him to take more ground at a rack-rent that was more than any Christian ought to pay to another, seeing there was no making it. When my father—and small blame to him for that—refused to lease the ground, he turned us off the bit of land we had, and out of the house and all, and left us in a wide and wicked world, where my father, for he was a soft innocent man, was not up to the roguery and the trickery that was practised upon him. He was taken this way by one and that way by another, and he treating them that were working his downfall. And he used to take bite and sup with them, and they with him, free enough as long as the money lasted; but when that was gone, and he had not as much ground, that he could call his own, as would sod a lark, they soon shabbed him off. The landlord died not long after; and he now knows whether he acted right or wrong in taking the house from over our heads.

"It is a bad thing for the heart to be cast down, so we took another cabin, and looked out with great desire for the Fir darrig to come to us. But ten o'clock came, and no arm, although we cut a hole in the door just the *moral* (model) of the other. Eleven o'clock!—twelve o'clock!—no, not a sign of him: and every night we watched, but all would not do. We then travelled to the other house, and we rooted up the hearth, for the landlord asked so great a rent for it from the poor people that no one could take it; and we carried away the very door off the hinges, and we brought every thing with us that we thought the little man was in any respect partial to, but he did not come, and we never saw him again.

"My father and my mother, and my young sister, are since dead, and my two brothers, who could tell all about this better than myself, are both of them gone out with Ingram in his last voyage to the Cape of Good Hope, leaving me behind without kith or kin."

Here young Ellen's voice became choked with sorrow, and bursting into tears, she hid her face in her apron.

This tale is preserved verbatim as taken down by Mr. M'Clise, to whose clever pencil the present volume is also indebted for the idea of two or three of the sketches which illustrate it.

The Fir darrig here has many traits of resemblance with the Scotch Brownie, the German Kobold, and the Hob-goblin of England (Milton's "Lubber fiend.") They all love cleanliness and regularity, are harbingers of good-luck, and in general, for some exceptions occur, are like cats, attached to the house rather than to the family.

Crogh-na-drimina bog lies at the foot of Cairn Thierna, near Fermoy, a hill which is the scene of a subsequent story.

Cough-na-Looba's dance with the black friar at Rahill, as well as the legend of the Dead Man's Hollow, are traditions well known in the county of Tipperary. The present worthy possessor of Rahill (Mr. Fennell, a Quaker gentleman) can bear witness to the popular belief in Cough-na-Looba's existence, and her supposed abode in his orchard, where she is constantly heard singing

> "*Na feck a vecetoo*
> *Na clush a glushetoo*
> *Na nish gevacketoo*
> *Cough a na Looba.*"

The fair dame's song is given as it is pronounced, and has been translated to the writer by a singular character named Cleary, whose *soubriquet* was "The Wild Fox," as follows:

> Don't see what you see,
> Don't hear what you hear,
> Don't tell what you saw
> Of Cathèrine Looby.

"The Drutheen," which is supposed to possess the power of revealing the name of a sweetheart, is a small white slug or naked snail, and it is the common practice of boys and maids on May morning to place one on a piece of slate lightly sprinkled with flour or fine dust, covering it over with a large leaf, when it never fails to describe the initial of "the one loved name."

The same custom prevailed in England in the time of Gay, and is described by him in "The Shepherd's Week."

> "Last May-day fair I search'd to find a snail
> That might my secret lover's name reveal;
> Upon a gooseberry-bush a snail I found,
> For always snails near sweetest fruit abound.
> I seized the vermin, home I quickly sped,
> And on the hearth the milk-white embers spread.
> Slow crawl'd the snail, and if I right can spell,
> In the soft ashes mark'd a curious L:
> Oh, may this wond'rous omen lucky prove,
> For L is found in Lubberkin and Love."

The word is correctly written *drùchdan*, which signifies morning-dew, as, according to vulgar opinion, these snails fall with, and are born of the dew, and are never seen but when the dew is on the ground. A kind correspondent (Mr. Richard Dowden Richard) suggests, as a probable derivation, *Druàdh*, a magician, and hence *Druàdheen*, the little magician.

The flint arrow-heads of the primitive inhabitants, and the axes termed by antiquaries stone celts, are frequently found in turning up the ground in Ireland, as well as Scotland and other countries. By the peasantry they are termed elf-stones, and believed to have been maliciously shot at cattle by "the wandering people."

Thus Collins, in his beautiful ode on the superstitions of the Highlands

> "There every herd by sad experience knows
> How wing'd with fate their elf-shot arrows fly;
> When the sick ewe her summer-food foregoes,
> Or, stretch'd on earth, the heart-smit heifers lie."

It may appear rather hazardous to employ the word noways in the opening sentence of the tale, after the declaration of Dr. Johnson, who, in his derivation of *nowise*, says "this word is, by some ignorant barbarians, written and pronounced *noways.*" Few, however, now rate the authority of Dr. Johnson very high upon any subject, and in etymological ones it goes for nothing. Sir Walter Scott very slily remarks, when speaking of the greatest of the Jonsons, old Ben, that "he is not the only one of the name that has bullied his contemporaries into taking him at his own valuation;" but the man who wrote the Alchymist was certainly very far superior in every respect to the author of Irene.

We cannot venture decidedly to maintain that noways is the proper writing of the word, for we know that our Saxon ancestors more frequently employed piſe, *wise,* modus, than peᵹ, *way.* Thus we meet on nane piſan, *in nowise;* on oþre piſan, *otherwise;* on æniᵹe piſan, *in anywise;* on tpa, on tpeo piſan, *in two or three wise.* But we also meet Ealle pæᵹa, omnibus modis, and Ealne peᵹ, *always,* semper. And besides *always* we still use *straightways, lengthways,* and other similar adverbs, which would appear to indicate the former use of several adverbs formed from peᵹ in the regular Teutonic manner, that is, by a genitive termination. *Nowise* and *noways* is, in German, *keineswegs.* It is curious that the Saxon Eft ſona should have become *eftsoons.*

FAIRY LEGENDS.

TREASURE LEGENDS.

“ Bell, book, and candle, shall not drive me back
When gold and silver becks me to come on.”

KING JOHN.

“ This is fairy gold, boy, and ’twill prove so.”

WINTER’S TALE.

TREASURE LEGENDS.

DREAMING TIM JARVIS.

TIMOTHY Jarvis was a decent, honest, quiet, hard-working man, as every body knows that knows Balledehob.

Now Balledehob is a small place, about forty miles west of Cork. It is situated on the summit of a hill, and yet it is in a deep valley; for on all sides there are lofty mountains that rise one above another in barren grandeur, and seem to look down with scorn upon the little busy village, which they surround with their idle and unproductive magnificence. Man and beast have alike deserted them to the dominion of the eagle, who soars majestically over them. On the highest of those mountains there is a small, and as is commonly believed, unfathomable lake, the only inhabitant of which is a huge serpent, who has been sometimes seen to stretch its enormous head above the waters, and frequently is heard to utter a noise which shakes the very rocks to their foundation.

But, as I was saying, every body knew Tim Jarvis to be a decent, honest, quiet, hard-working man, who was thriving enough to be able to give his daughter Nelly a fortune of ten pounds; and Tim himself would have been snug enough besides, but that he loved the drop sometimes. However, he was seldom backward on rent day. His ground was never distrained but twice, and both times through a small bit of a mistake; and his landlord had never but once to say to him—"Tim Jarvis, you 're all behind, Tim, like the cow's tail." Now it so happened that, being heavy in himself, through the drink, Tim took to sleeping, and the sleep set Tim dreaming, and he dreamed all night, and night after night, about crocks full of gold and other precious stones; so much so, that Norah Jarvis his wife could get no good of him by day, and have little comfort with him by night. The grey dawn of the morning would see Tim digging away in a bog-hole, maybe, or rooting under some old stone walls like a pig. At last he dreamt that he found a mighty great crock of gold and silver—and where, do you think? Every step of the way upon London-bridge, itself! Twice Tim dreamt it, and three times Tim dreamt the same thing; and at last he made up his mind to transport himself, and go over to London, in Pat Mahoney's coaster—and so he did!

Well, he got there, and found the bridge without much difficulty. Every day he walked up and down looking for the crock of gold, but never the find did he find it. One day, however, as he was looking over the bridge into the water, a man, or something like a man, with great black whiskers, like a Hessian, and a black cloak that reached down to the ground, taps him on the shoulder, and says he—"Tim Jarvis, do you see me?"

"Surely I do, sir," said Tim; wondering that any body should know him in the strange place.

"Tim," says he, "what is it brings you here in foreign parts, so far away from your own cabin by the mine of grey copper at Balledehob?"

"Please your honour," says Tim, "I'm come to seek my fortune."

"You're a fool for your pains, Tim, if that's all," remarked the stranger in the black cloak; "this is a big place to seek one's fortune in, to be sure, but it's not so easy to find it."

Now, Tim, after debating a long time with himself, and considering, in the first place, that it might be the stranger who was to find the crock of gold for him; and in the next, that the stranger might direct him where to find it, came to the resolution of telling him all.

"There's many a one like me comes here seeking their fortunes," said Tim.

"True," said the stranger.

"But," continued Tim, looking up, "the body and bones of the cause for myself leaving the woman, and Nelly, and the boys, and travelling so far, is to look for a crock of gold that I 'm told is lying somewhere hereabouts."

"And who told you that, Tim?"

"Why, then, sir, that 's what I can't tell myself rightly—only I dreamt it."

"Ho, ho! is that all, Tim?" said the stranger, laughing; "I had a dream myself; and I dreamed that I found a crock of gold, in the Fort field, on Jerry Driscoll's ground at Balledehob; and by the same token, the pit where it lay was close to a large furze bush, all full of yellow blossom."

Tim knew Jerry Driscoll's ground well; and, moreover, he knew the fort field as well as he knew his own potatoe garden; he was certain, too, of the very furze bush at the north end of it—so, swearing a bitter big oath, says he—

"By all the crosses in a yard of check, I always thought there was money in that same field!"

The moment he rapped out the oath the stranger disappeared, and Tim Jarvis, wondering at all that had happened to him, made the best of his way back to Ireland. Norah, as may well be supposed, had no very warm welcome for her runaway husband—the dreaming blackguard, as she called him—and so soon as she set eyes upon him, all the blood of her body in one minute was into her knuckles to be at him; but Tim, after his long journey, looked so cheerful and so happy-like, that she could not find it in her heart to give him the first blow! He managed to pacify his wife by two or three broad hints about a new cloak and a pair of shoes, that, to speak honestly, were much wanting to her to go to chapel in; and decent clothes for Nelly to go to the patron with her sweetheart, and brogues for the boys, and some corduroy for himself. "It wasn't for nothing," says Tim, "I went to foreign parts all the ways; and you 'll see what 'll come out of it—mind my words."

A few days afterwards Tim sold his cabin and his garden, and bought the fort field of Jerry Driscoll, that had nothing in it, but was full of thistles, and old stones, and blackberry bushes; and all the neighbours—as well they might—thought he was cracked!

The first night that Tim could summon courage to begin his work, he walked off to the field with his spade upon his shoulder; and away he dug all night by the side of the furze bush, till he came to a big stone. He struck his spade against it, and he heard a hollow sound; but as the morning had begun to dawn, and the neighbours would be going out to their work, Tim, not wishing to have the thing talked about, went home to the little hovel, where Norah and the children were huddled together under a heap of straw; for he had sold every thing he had in the world to purchase Driscoll's field, that was said to be "the back-bone of the world, picked by the devil."

It is impossible to describe the epithets and reproaches bestowed by the poor woman on her unlucky husband for bringing her into such a way. Epithets and reproaches which Tim had but one mode of answering, as thus:—"Norah, did you see e'er a cow you'd like?"—or, "Norah, dear, hasn't Poll Deasy a feather-bed to sell?"—or, "Norah, honey, wouldn't you like your silver buckles as big as Mrs. Doyle's?"

As soon as night came Tim stood beside the furze bush spade in hand. The moment he jumped down into the pit he heard a strange rumbling noise under him, and so, putting his ear against the great stone, he listened, and overheard a discourse that made the hair on his head stand up like bulrushes, and every limb tremble.

"How shall we bother Tim?" said one voice.

"Take him to the mountain, to be sure, and make him a toothful for the old serpent; 'tis long since he has had a good meal," said another voice.

Tim shook like a potatoe-blossom in a storm.

"No," said a third voice; "plunge him in the bog, neck and heels."

Tim was a dead man, barring the breath *.

"Stop!" said a fourth; but Tim heard no more, for Tim was dead entirely. In about an hour, however, the life came back into him, and he crept home to Norah.

When the next night arrived the hopes of the crock of gold got the better of his fears, and taking care to arm himself with a bottle of potheen, away he went to the field. Jumping into the pit, he took a little sup from the bottle to keep his heart up—he then took a big one—and then, with desperate wrench, he wrenched up the stone. All at once, up rushed a blast of wind, wild and fierce, and down fell Tim—down, down, and down he went —until he thumped upon what seemed to be, for all the world, like a floor of sharp pins, which made him bellow out in earnest. Then he heard a whisk and a hurra, and instantly voices beyond number cried out—

> "Welcome, Tim Jarvis, dear!
> Welcome, down here!"

---

* "I' non morì, e non rimasi vivo:
Pensa oramai per te, s' hai fior d' ingegno
Qual io divenni d' uno e d' altro privo."

DANTE INFERNO, Canto 34.

Though Tim's teeth chattered like magpies with the fright, he continued to make answer—" I'm he-he-har-ti-ly ob-ob-liged to-to you all, gen-gentlemen, fo-for your civility to-to a poor stranger like myself." But though he had heard all the voices about him, he could see nothing, the place was so dark and so lonesome in itself for want of the light. Then something pulled Tim by the hair of his head, and dragged him, he did not know how far, but he knew he was going faster than the wind, for he heard it behind him, trying to keep up with him, and it could not. On, on, on, he went, till all at once, and suddenly, he was stopped, and somebody came up to him, and said, " Well, Tim Jarvis, and how do you like your ride?"

" Mighty well! I thank your honour," said Tim; " and 'twas a good beast I rode, surely!"

There was a great laugh at Tim's answer; and then there was a whispering, and a great cugger mugger, and coshering; and at last a pretty little bit of a voice said, " Shut your eyes, and you 'll see, Tim."

" By my word, then," said Tim, " that is the queer way of seeing; but I 'm not the man to gainsay you, so I 'll do as you bid me, any how." Presently he felt a small warm hand rubbed over his eyes with an ointment, and in the next minute he saw himself in the middle of thousands of little men and women, not half so high as his brogue, that were pelting one another with golden guineas and lily-white thirteens*, as if they were so much dirt. The finest dressed and the biggest of them all went up to Tim, and says he, "Tim Jarvis, because you are a decent, honest, quiet, civil, well-spoken man," says he, "and know how to behave yourself in strange company, we've altered our minds about you, and will find a neighbour of yours that will do just as well to give to the old serpent."

"Oh, then, long life to you, sir!" said Tim, "and there's no doubt of that."

"But what will you say, Tim," inquired the little fellow, "if we fill your pockets with these yellow boys? What will you say, Tim, and what will you do with them?"

"Your honour's honour, and your honour's glory," answered Tim, "I'll not be able to say my prayers for one month with thanking you—and indeed I've enough to do with them. I'd make a grand lady, you see, at once of Norah—she has been a good wife to me. We'll have a nice bit of pork for dinner; and, maybe, I'd have a glass, or maybe two glasses; or sometimes, if

* An English shilling was thirteen pence Irish currency.

'twas with a friend, or acquaintance, or gossip, you know, three glasses every day; and I 'd build a new cabin; and I 'd have a fresh egg every morning, myself, for my breakfast; and I 'd snap my fingers at the 'squire, and beat his hounds, if they 'd come coursing through my fields; and I 'd have a new plough; and Norah, your honour, should have a new cloak, and the boys should have shoes and stockings as well as Biddy Leary's brats —that 's my sister what was—and Nelly should marry Bill Long of Affadown; and, your honour, I'd have some corduroy for myself to make breeches, and a cow, and a beautiful coat with shining buttons, and a horse to ride, or maybe two. I'd have every thing," said Tim, "in life, good or bad, that is to be got for love or money—hurra-whoop!— and that 's what I 'd do."

"Take care, Tim," said the little fellow, "your money would not go faster than it came, with your hurra-whoop."

But Tim heeded not this speech: heaps of gold were around him, and he filled and filled away as hard as he could, his coat and his waistcoat and his breeches pockets; and he thought himself very clever, moreover, because he stuffed some of the guineas into his brogues. When the little people perceived this, they cried out—"Go home, Tim Jarvis, go home, and think yourself a lucky man."

"I hope, gentlemen," said he, "we won't part for good and all; but maybe ye'll ask me to see you again, and to give you a fair and square account of what I've done with your money."

To this there was no answer, only another shout—"Go home, Tim Jarvis—go home—fair play is a jewel; but shut your eyes, or ye'll never see the light of day again."

Tim shut his eyes, knowing now that was the way to see clearly; and away he was whisked as before—away, away he went 'till he again stopped all of a sudden.

He rubbed his eyes with his two thumbs—and where was he?—Where, but in the very pit in the field that was Jer Driscoll's, and his wife Norah above with a big stick ready to beat "her dreaming blackguard." Tim roared out to the woman to leave the life in him, and put his hands in his pockets to show her the gold; but he pulled out nothing only a handful of small stones mixed with yellow furze blossoms. The bush was under him, and the great flag-stone that he had wrenched up, as he thought, was lying, as if it was never stirred, by his side: the whiskey bottle was drained to the last drop; and the pit was just as his spade had made it.

Tim Jarvis, vexed, disappointed, and almost

heart-broken, followed his wife home: and, strange to say, from that night he left off drinking, and dreaming, and delving in bog-holes, and rooting in old caves. He took again to his hard working habits, and was soon able to buy back his little cabin and former potato-garden, and to get all the enjoyment he anticipated from the fairy gold.

Give Tim one or, at most, two glasses of whiskey punch (and neither friend, acquaintance, or gossip can make him take more), and he will relate the story to you much better than you have it here. Indeed it is worth going to Balledehob to hear him tell it. He always pledges himself to the truth of every word with his fore-fingers crossed; and when he comes to speak of the loss of his guineas, he never fails to console himself by adding —"If they staid with me I wouldn't have luck with them, sir; and father O'Shea told me 'twas as well for me they were changed, for if they hadn't, they'd have burned holes in my pocket, and got out that way."

I shall never forget his solemn countenance, and the deep tones of his warning voice, when he concluded his tale, by telling me, that the next day after his ride with the fairies, Mick Dowling was missing, and he believed him to be given to the serpent in his place, as he had never been heard of since. "The blessing of the saints be between all good men and harm," was the concluding sentence of Tim Jarvis's narrative, as he flung the remaining drops from his glass upon the green sward.

In Grimm's Deutsche Sagan (vol. i. p. 290) this tale, which is also current, with little variation, in the East, is thus related :—" A man once dreamed that if he went to Regensburg and walked on the bridge he should become rich. He went accordingly; and when he had spent near a fortnight walking backwards and forwards on the bridge, a rich merchant came up to him, wondering what he was doing there every day, and asked him what he was looking for; he answered that he had dreamed if he would go to the bridge of Regensburg he should become rich. 'Ah!' said the merchant, 'what do you say about dreams?—Dreams are but froth (*Träume sind Schäume*). I too have dreamed that there is buried under yonder large tree (pointing to it) a great kettle full of money; but I give no heed to this, for dreams are froth' (*Träume sind Schäume*).

"The man went immediately and dug under the tree, and there he got a great treasure, which made a rich man of him; and so his dream was accomplished.

"This story," says Agricola, "I have often heard

from my father. The same story is told of several other places. At Lubeck it was a baker's boy who dreamed he should find a treasure on the bridge. On the bridge he met a beggar, who said he had dreamed there was one under a lime-tree in the church-yard of Möllen, but that he would not take the trouble of going there. The baker's boy went and got the treasure."

Precisely the same legend is recorded in the Danske Folkesagn (vol. ii. p. 24), of a man at a place called Als, who dreamed he should find a treasure in the streets of Flensborg, and was directed back to Tanslet near Als. But perhaps there is no country in which this story is not current.

Should any reader be fortunate enough to dream of buried money, it may be of some advantage to know the proper "art and order" to be used in digging for it.

"There must be made upon a hazel wand three crosses, and certain words, both blasphemous and impious, must be said over it; and hereunto must be added certain characters and barbarous names. And whilst the treasure is a-digging, there must be read the psalms *De profundis, Misereatur nostri, Requiem, Pater noster, Ave Maria, Et ne nos inducas in tentationem, sed libera nos a malo, Amen, A porta inferni credo videre bona, &c.*, and then a certain prayer. And if the time of digging be neglected the devil will carry all the treasure away." *Reg. Scot. Discoverie of Witchcraft, p.* 102.

All money-diggers, however, ought to take warning

by the fate of one recorded in Dodsley's Annual Register for 1774.

"Daniel Healey of Donoghmore, in Ireland, having three different times dreamed that money lay concealed under a large stone in a field near where he lived, procured some workmen to assist him in removing it; and when they had dug as far as the foundation, it suddenly fell and killed Healey on the spot."

RENT-DAY.

"OH ullagone, ullagone! this is a wide world, but what will we do in it, or where will we go?" muttered Bill Doody, as he sat on a rock by the Lake of Killarney. "What will we do? to-morrow 's rent-day, and Tim the Driver swears if we don't pay up our rent, he 'll cant every *ha'perth* we have; and then, sure enough, there 's Judy and myself, and the poor little *grawls* * will be turned out to starve on the high road, for the never a halfpenny of rent have I!—Oh hone, that ever I should live to see this day!"

Thus did Bill Doody bemoan his hard fate, pouring his sorrows to the reckless waves of the most beautiful of lakes, which seemed to mock his misery as they rejoiced beneath the cloudless sky of a May morning. That lake, glittering in sun-shine, sprinkled with fairy isles of rock and ver-dure, and bounded by giant hills of ever-varying

* Children.

hues, might, with its magic beauty, charm all sadness but despair; for alas,

> "How ill the scene that offers rest
> And heart that cannot rest agree!"

Yet Bill Doody was not so desolate as he supposed; there was one listening to him he little thought of, and help was at hand from a quarter he could not have expected.

"What's the matter with you, my poor man?" said a tall portly-looking gentleman, at the same time stepping out of a furze brake. Now Bill was seated on a rock that commanded the view of a large field. Nothing in the field could be concealed from him, except this furze-brake, which grew in a hollow near the margin of the lake. He was, therefore, not a little surprised at the gentleman's sudden appearance, and began to question whether the personage before him belonged to this world or not. He, however, soon mustered courage sufficient to tell him how his crops had failed, how some bad member had charmed away his butter, and how Tim the Driver threatened to turn him out of the farm if he didn't pay up every penny of the rent by twelve o'clock next day.

"A sad story, indeed," said the stranger; "but

surely, if you represented the case to your landlord's agent, he won't have the heart to turn you out."

"Heart, your honour! where would an agent get a heart!" exclaimed Bill. "I see your honour does not know him; besides, he has an eye on the farm this long time for a fosterer of his own; so I expect no mercy at all, at all, only to be turned out."

"Take this, my poor fellow, take this," said the stranger, pouring a purse full of gold into Bill's old hat, which in his grief he had flung on the ground. "Pay the fellow your rent, but I'll take care it shall do him no good. I remember the time when things went otherwise in this country, when I would have hung up such a fellow in the twinkling of an eye!"

These words were lost upon Bill, who was insensible to every thing but the sight of the gold, and before he could unfix his gaze, and lift up his head to pour out his hundred thousand blessings, the stranger was gone. The bewildered peasant looked around in search of his benefactor, and at last he thought he saw him riding on a white horse a long way off on the lake.

"O'Donoghue, O'Donoghue!" shouted Bill; "the good, the blessed O'Donoghue!" and he ran capering like a madman to show Judy the gold, and to rejoice her heart with the prospect of wealth and happiness.

The next day Bill proceeded to the agent's; not sneakingly, with his hat in his hand, his eyes fixed on the ground, and his knees bending under him; but bold and upright, like a man conscious of his independence.

"Why don't you take off your hat, fellow; don't you know you are speaking to a magistrate?" said the agent.

"I know I'm not speaking to the king, sir," said Bill; "and I never takes off my hat but to them I can respect and love. The Eye that sees all knows I've no right either to respect or love an agent!"

"You scoundrel!" retorted the man in office, biting his lips with rage at such an unusual and unexpected opposition, "I'll teach you how to be insolent again—I have the power, remember."

"To the cost of the country, I know you have," said Bill, who still remained with his head as firmly covered as if he was the lord Kingsale himself.

"But, come," said the magistrate; "have you got the money for me?—this is rent-day. If there's one penny of it wanting, or the running gale that's due, prepare to turn out before night, for you shall not remain another hour in possession.

"There is your rent," said Bill, with an unmoved expression of tone and countenance; "you 'd better count it, and give me a receipt in full for the running gale and all."

The agent gave a look of amazement at the gold; for it was gold—real guineas! and not bits of dirty ragged small notes, that are only fit to light one's pipe with. However willing the agent may have been to ruin, as he thought, the unfortunate tenant, he took up the gold, and handed the receipt to Bill, who strutted off with it as proud as a cat of her whiskers.

The agent going to his desk shortly after, was confounded at beholding a heap of gingerbread cakes instead of the money he had deposited there. He raved and swore, but all to no purpose; the gold had become gingerbread cakes, just marked like the guineas, with the king's head, and Bill had the receipt in his pocket; so he saw there was no use in saying any thing about the affair, as he would only get laughed at for his pains.

From that hour Bill Doody grew rich; all his undertakings prospered; and he often blesses the day that he met with O'Donoghue, the great prince that lives down under the lake of Killarney.

Another legend respecting the appearance of O'Donoghue is given in the preceding volume, where, to use the words of Miss Luby, (the fair minstrel of Killarney,)

> " Aerial spirits in a heavenly throng
> Skim the blue waves, and follow him along."
> *Spirit of the Lakes,* c. ii.

When at Killarney in the spring of 1825, the writer received the following accounts of the appearance of O'Donoghue from actual spectators. The first from a man who was employed in the mines at Ross about twelve or thirteen years before, when colonel Hall had carried an excavation under the lake, which invasion of his dominions was popularly considered to be extremely offensive to O'Donoghue.

" I saw him, sir," he continued, " early in the morning, when the water broke into the mines, sweeping all before it like a raging sea, and made the workmen fly for their lives. It was just at daybreak that morning I saw him on the lake, followed by numbers of men mounted upon horseback like *carvally* (cavalry), and each having a drawn sword as bright as the day in his right hand, and a *carbuncle* (carbine) slung at the side of himself and his horse; a thing like a great tent came down from the sky, and covered them all over, and when it cleared away nothing more of O'Donoghue or his men was to be seen."

The other account was given by a boatman usually called (from his familiarity with the great chieftain)

O'Donoghue, but whose real name was Edward Doolin; and the accuracy of his statement is confirmed by Tim Lyne, the old coxswain.

"Ten years ago we went out about seven o'clock in the morning to make a long day on the lakes; the water was calm and the sun was shining bright, and it was just nine o'clock when we saw O'Donoghue going from the 'half-moon' of Toomies round Rabbit Island. He was dressed in white, with a cocked-hat, and shoes with great buckles in them, and he walked very smart on the water, spattering it up before him; James Curtin, who pulled the bow oar, saw him, too, for as good as seven minutes, and he is alive and able to speak the truth as well as myself. We had two gentlemen in the boat at the time. One of them was a counsellor Moore from Dublin, and they made great wonder at the sight. O'Donoghue, when he finds poor travellers benighted, who are coming for Killarney, takes them down into his palace below the lake, where he entertains them grandly without their paying any cost. The white horse that he sometimes rides, and whose image is in a rock upon the lake, is called *Crebough*."

The circulation of money bestowed by the fairies or supernatural personages, like that of counterfeit coin, is seldom extensive. The story in the Arabian Nights, of the old rogue whose fine-looking money turned to leaves, must be familiar to every reader. When Waldemar, Holger, and Grœn Jette, in Danish tradition, bestow money upon the Boors whom they meet, their gift sometimes turns to fire, sometimes to pebbles, and sometimes is so hot, that the receiver drops it from his hand, when the gold, or what seemed to be so, sinks into the ground and disappears. In some cases these changes take place as in the foregoing tale, after the Boors have parted with their money. If a piece of coal, or any thing in appearance equally valueless, is given, it always, if kept, proves to be gold. The travelling musicians, who had the honour to play before the enchanted German emperor, Frederick, in the mountain in which he resides, were each rewarded by the monarch with a green branch. Highly incensed at such shabby wages, they all except one flung away the gift, and went out of the mountain. One minstrel, however, who kept his branch found it growing heavy in his hand, and on examination he discovered that it was composed of pure gold. His companions immediately went back to look for those which they had thrown away, but their branches were not to be found.

SCATH-A-LEGAUNE.

"WELL, for sure and certain, there must be something in it," said Johnny Curtin, as he awoke and stretched himself one fine morning, "for certain there must be something in it, or he'd never have come the third time. Troth and faith, as I can't do it myself without help, I'll just speak to the master about it, for half a loaf is better than no bread any day in the year."

Johnny Curtin was a poor scholar; he had been stopping for the last week at the house of Dick Cassidy, a snug farmer, who lived not far from the fine old abbey of Holy Cross, in the county of Tipperary. Mr. Cassidy was a hearty man, and loved a story in his soul; and Johnny Curtin had as good a budget of old songs, and stories of every kind and sort, as any poor scholar that ever carried an ink-bottle dangling at his breast, or a well-thumbed book and a slate under his arm. He was, moreover, as good a man in a hay-field, for a boy of his years, as need to be, so that no one was a more welcome guest to Dick Cassidy in harvest time than Johnny Curtin.

The third night after Johnny had taken up his

quarters at Cassidy's farm-house, after sitting up very late, and telling his most wonderful stories to Dick and the children, Johnny went to sleep on a shake-down (of straw) in a corner, and there he dreamed a dream. For he thought that an old man, with a fine long beard, and dressed from head to foot in the real old ancient Irish fashion, came and stood beside him, and called him by his name.

"Johnny Curtin, my child," said the old man, "do you know where you are?"

"I do, sir," said Johnny, though great was his surprise. "I do, sir," said he; "I am at Dick Cassidy's."

"John, do you know," says he, "that this land belonged, in the good old times, to your own people?"

"Oh I'm sure," says Johnny, "it's little myself knows about my own people, beyond my father and my mother, who, when one would catch the fish, the other would sell it; but this I know, if 'tis as your honour says, and not doubting your word in the least, that I wish my own people had kept their land, that I might have got the *larning* without begging for it from door to door through the country."

"John," said the old man, "there's a treasure not far from this that belonged to the family, and if you get it, it will make you, and fifty like you, as rich as kings. Now, mind my words, John Curtin, for I have come to put you in the right way. You know the height above the abbey—the blessed spot where the piece of the holy cross fell from its concealment at the sweet sound of the abbey bells, and where the good woman met her son, after his having travelled to Jerusalem for it? You know the old bush that is standing there—*Scath-a-legaune*—in the bleak situation, close to the road, upon the little bank of earth and stones? dig just six feet from it, in a line with the tower of the old abbey; the work must be done in the dead hour of the night, and not a word must be spoken to living man."

When Johnny woke next morning he recollected every part of his dream well, but he gave no great heed to it. The next night he dreamed that the same old man came to him again and spoke the very same words; and in the course of the day following, he could not help going up to Scath-a-legaune, to take a look at the old bush and the little bank of stones and earth, but still he thought it all nonsense going digging there. At last, when the old man came to him in his sleep the third time, and seemed rather angry with him, he resolved to broach the matter to Dick after breakfast, and see if he would join him in the search.

Now Dick Cassidy, like many wiser men, was a firm believer in dreams; and Dick was also a prudent man, and willing to better himself and his family in any honest way, so he gave at once into Johnny's proposal, that they should both go the next night and dig under the bush. When Cassidy mentioned this scheme to Peggy his wife, she being a religious woman, was much against it, and wanted Dick not to go, and tried to persuade him to take neither hand, nor act, nor part in it; but Dick was too sensible a man, and too fond of his own way, to be said by any foolish woman: so it was settled, that at twelve o'clock he and Johnny Curtin should take spade, pick-axe, and crow-bar with them, and set out for the bush, having agreed to divide fairly between them whatever they should get.

After a good supper, and a stiff jug of punch to keep their hearts up, Mr. Cassidy and Johnny Curtin, regardless of the admonitions of Peggy, set out. They had to pass close under the walls of the old abbey, and the wind, which was rather high, kept flapping the branches of the ash and ivy backwards and forwards, and now and then some of the old stones would tumble down, and the boughs would move and creak with a sound just like the voice of some Christian that was in pain.

Dick and Johnny, with all their courage, were not much assured at hearing this; but they did not remain very long to listen, and crossing the bridge with all convenient speed, directed their steps towards Scath-a-legaune. When they got to the old bush, Dick, without a moment's delay, threw off his coat, stepped the six feet of ground from the little bank towards the tower of the abbey, and began to turn up the sod, and then to dig hard and fast. Johnny all the time stood by, praying to himself, and making pious signs on his forehead and breast. When Dick had dug for better than an hour, he found his spade strike against something hard. He cleared out the loose earth from the hole he had made, and then found that he had come to a great broad flag-stone which was lying quite flat: he saw plainly that he and Johnny could no more lift it than they could fling the rock of Cashel back again into the Devil's bit; so he got up out of the hole and made motions to Johnny Curtin, minding well not to speak a word; and they threw in part of the clay to cover up the flag, and went home to bed planning to get more help against the next night, and fully convinced of success.

The next day Cassidy pitched on three of his best and stoutest men, and in the evening early took them down to the sign of the Saint *, kept by one Mullowney in the village, and proposed the job to them, after giving each a rummer of Roscrea †. They hesitated at the first, saying it was not lucky, and they never heard of good that came out of money that was got at through the means of dreams, and so on, until Dick ordered a second rummer for every man: then he made Johnny tell them his dream over again from beginning to end, and he asked them, if they could see any reason upon earth to doubt what Johnny Curtin told them, or that the old man came to him through his sleep, and he able to mention every pin's worth of his dress. Dick argued with them in this manner, saying a thousand things more of the same kind, until they made an end of their drink, and then he made an offer of giving them a fair share of whatever money was under the flag-stone.

The men at last were over-persuaded; and between eleven and twelve they set out, provided with spades, shovels, and good crow-bars. When they came to the rise of the height, Johnny stopped, and again told them that all their work was sure to fail if any one spoke a word; and he said that silence must be kept, let what would happen, otherwise there was no chance of making out the trea-

* Patrick. † Whiskey.

sure that beyond all doubt was lying there buried down in the ground.

They cleared away the earth from off the stone, and got the crow-bars under it. The first prize they gave they thought they heard a rumbling noise below: they stopped and listened for a minute or more, but all was silent as the grave. Again they heaved, and there was a noise like as if a door was clapped to violently. The men hesitated, but Dick Cassidy and Johnny, by signs, encouraged them to go on. They then made a great effort and raised the stone a little, while Johnny and Tom Doyle wedged in the handles of their spades, and with their united strength the flag was canted fairly over.

Beneath there was a long flight of steps, so they lit a piece of candle which they had brought with them, and down the steps they went, one after the other. The steps, when they got to the end of them, led into a long passage, that went some way, and there they would have been stopped by a strong door, only it was half open. They went in boldly, and saw another door to the left, which was shut. There was a little grate in this door, and Dick Cassidy held up the light while Ned Flaherty looked in.

"Hurra!" cried Ned, the minute he put his eye to the bars, and straightways making a blow at the door, with the crow-bar in his hand—"Hurra, boys!" says he; "by Noonan's ghost! we are all made men!"

The words had hardly passed his lips when there was a tremendous crashing noise, just as if the whole place was falling in, and then came a screeching wind from the inner room that whisked out the light, and threw them all on the ground flat on their faces. When they recovered themselves they hardly remembered where they were, or what had happened, and they had lost all the geography of the place. They groped and tumbled about for a long time, and at last they got, with falling and roaring, to the door where they had come in at, and made their way up the steps into the field. On looking towards the abbey, there was a bright flame on the top of its tower, and Bill Dunn would have sworn he saw a figure of something, he could not rightly make out what, in the middle of it, dancing up and down.

Frightened enough they were at the sight, for they plainly perceived something was going on which they could not understand, so they made the best of their way home; but it was little any of them could sleep, as may well be supposed, after what had happened.

Next morning they all held a council about what was further to be done—Mr. Cassidy and Johnny

Curtin, Tom Doyle, and Bill Dunn, and Ned Flaherty, whose tongue was the reason of their not being all rich men. Some were for giving the business up entirely, but more were for trying it again; and at last Dick Cassidy said he was resolved to go to it the third time, since he was now certain the coin was there; for Ned Flaherty swore he saw a mint of money, beside gold and silver vessels in heaps, and other grand things that he could not tell the use of. It was settled, however, to do nothing the next night.

In the middle of the day Dick took Johnny with him, and walked over to look at the place where they had been digging; but what was their astonishment to find the ground as smooth and as even as if there had not been a spade put into it since the days of Brian Boro! Not a morsel of clay was to be seen, and the white daisies and the glossy yellow butter-cups were growing up through the green grass as gaily there, as if nothing had ever happened to disturb them.

That night Johnny Curtin had another dream. The very same old man came to him, and looked dark and angry at him for not having followed his directions; and told Johnny that he had no right to think, and that if his *larning* made him think he was better without it, he had lost all chance of growing rich, and would be a poor scholar to the end of his days; for the place was now shut up for another hundred years, and that it would be dangerous for him or any one else to go digging there until that time was out.

The stories about treasure, which has been discovered through spiritual agency, or that of dreams, are so numerous that, if collected, many volumes might be filled with them; yet they vary little in their details, beyond the actors and localities.

The following legends, two of which are translated from the Danish, will sufficiently prove this assertion, although they illustrate nearly the extreme variations:

There are still to be seen near Flensborg the ruins of a very ancient building. Two soldiers once stood on guard there together; but when one of them was gone to the town, it chanced that a tall white woman came to the other, and spoke to him, and said, I am an unhappy spirit, who have wandered here these many hundred years, but never shall I find rest in the grave. She then informed him, that under the walls of the castle a great treasure was concealed, which only three men in the whole world could take up, and that he was one of the three. The man, who now saw that his fortune was made, promised to follow her directions in every particular, whereupon she desired him to come to the same place at twelve o'clock the following night

The other soldier meanwhile had come back from the town, just as the appointment was made with his comrade. He said nothing about what unseen he had seen and heard, but went early the next evening, and concealed himself among some bushes. When his fellow-soldier came with his spade and shovel he found the white woman at the appointed place, but when she perceived that they were watched she put off the business till the next evening. The man who had lain on the watch to no purpose, went home, and suddenly fell ill; and as he thought that he should die of that sickness, he sent for his comrade, and told him how he knew all, and conjured him not to have any thing to do with witches or with spirits, but rather to seek counsel of the priest, who was a prudent man. The other thought it would be his wisest plan to follow the advice of his comrade, so he went and discovered the whole affair to the priest, who, however, desired him to do as the spirit had bid him, only to make her lay the first hand to the work herself.

The appointed time was now arrived, and the man was at the place. When the white woman had pointed out to him the spot, and they were just beginning the work, she said to him, that when the treasure was taken up, one half of it should be his, but that he must divide the other half equally between the church and the poor. Then the devil entered into the man, and awakened his covetousness, so that he cried out, "What! shall I not have the whole?" But scarcely had he spoken, when the figure, with a most mournful wail, passed in a blue flame over the moat of the castle, and the man fell sick, and died within three days.

The story soon spread through the country, and a poor scholar who heard it thought he had now an opportunity of making his fortune. He therefore went at midnight to the place, and there he met with the wandering white woman; and he told her why he was come, and offered his services to raise the treasure. But she answered him that he was not one of the three, one of whom alone could free her; and that the wall would still remain so firm, that no human being should be able to break it. She further told him, that at some future time he should be rewarded for his good inclination. And it is said, that when a long time after he passed by that place, and thought with compassion on the sufferings of the unblest woman, he fell on his face over a great heap of money, which soon put him again on his feet. But the wall still stands undisturbed; and as often as any one has attempted to throw it down, whatever is thrown down in the day is replaced again in the night.—*Danske Folkesagn*, vol. iv. p. 33.

Three men went once, in the night-time, to Klumhöi, to try their luck, for a dragon watches there over a great treasure. They dug into the ground, giving each other a strict charge not to utter a word, whatever might happen, otherwise all their labour would be in vain. When they had dug pretty deep, their spades struck against a copper chest; they then made signs to one another, and all, with both hands, laid hold of a great copper ring that was on the top of the chest, and pulled up the treasure; but when they had just got it into their possession, one of them forgot the necessity of silence, and shouted out, "One pull more, and we have it!" That very instant the chest flew away out of their hands to the lake of Stöierup, but as they all held hard on the ring it remained in their grasp. They went and fastened the ring on the door of St. Olai's church, and there it remains to this very day.—*Danske Folkesagn*, vol. i. p. 112.

"In the next country to that of my former residence," says Kirke, in his Secret Commonwealth, "about the year 1676, when there was some scarcity of grain, a marvellous illapse and vision strongly struck the imagination of two women in one night, living at a good distance from one another, about a treasure hid in a hill, called *Sithbhenaich*, or fairy hill. The appearance of a treasure was first represented to the fancy, and then an audible voice named the place where it was to their awaking senses. Whereupon, both arose, and meeting accidentally at the place discovered their design, and jointly digging, found a vessel as large as a Scottish peck full of small pieces of good money of ancient coin, which halving betwixt them, they sold in dishfulls for dishfulls of meal to the country-people. Very many of undoubted credit saw and had of the coin to this day. But whether it was a good or bad angel, one of the subterranean people, or the soul of him who hid it that discovered it, and to what end it was done, I leave to the examination of others."—P. 12.

The appearance of the tower of Holy Cross Abbey on fire is a common supernatural illusion. Another illustration is offered from the Danske Folkesagn, which may be acceptable, as Mr. Thiele's curious work is little known to the English reader.

"Near Daugstrup there is a hill which is called Daugbjerg Dous. Of this hill it is related that it is at all times covered with a blue mist, and that under it there lies a large copper kettle full of money. One night two men went there to dig after this treasure, and they had got so far as to have laid hold of the handle of the kettle. All sorts of wonderful things began then to appear to disturb them in their work. One time a coach, drawn by four black horses, drove by them; then they saw a black dog with a fiery tongue, then there came a cock drawing a load of hay. But still the men persisted in not letting themselves be induced to speak, and still dug on without stopping. At last a fellow came limping by them and said, 'See, Daugstrup is on fire!' and when they looked towards the town, it appeared exactly as if the whole place was in a bright flame. Then at length one of them forgot to keep silence, and the moment he uttered an exclamation the treasure sunk deeper and deeper; and as often since as any attempt has been made to get it up, the Trolds have, by their spells and artifices, prevented its success."—Vol. iv. p. 56.

The neighbourhood of Holy Cross abounds in wonders. From the Cashel road the hill of Killough is pointed out to the traveller as *Gardeen a Herin*, the garden of Ireland, in consequence of a belief that it is a national natural botanic establishment, and that every plant which grows in Ireland is to be found upon it. Not far from Scath-a-Legaune a small clear stream of water crosses the road from a spring called *Tubher-a-Doragh*, Doran's Well; whoever drinks at this fountain it is supposed will never feel the sensation of thirst, or a wish for water again. But there is really no end to tales of this kind.

LINN-NA-PAYSHTHA.

Travellers go to Leinster to see Dublin and the Dargle; to Ulster, to see the Giant's Causeway, and, perhaps, to do penance at Lough Dearg; to Munster, to see Killarney, the butter-buying city of Cork, and half a dozen other fine things; but whoever thinks of the fourth province?—whoever thinks of going—

> " — westward, where Dick Martin *ruled*
> The houseless wilds of Cunnemara?"

The Ulster-man's ancient denunciation "to Hell or to Connaught," has possibly led to the supposition that this is a sort of infernal place above ground—a kind of terrestrial Pandemonium—in short, that Connaught is little better than hell, or hell little worse than Connaught; but let any one only go there for a month, and, as the natives say, "I'll warrant he'll soon see the differ, and learn to understand that it is mighty like the rest o' green Erin, only something poorer;" and yet it might be thought that in this particular "worse would be needless;" but so it is.

"My gracious me," said the landlady of the Inn at Sligo, "I wonder a gentleman of your *teest* and *curosity* would think of leaving Ireland without making a *tower* (tour) of Connaught, if it was nothing more than spending a day at Hazlewood, and up the lake, and on to the *ould* abbey at Friarstown, and the castle at Dromahair."

Polly M'Bride, my kind hostess, might not in this remonstrance have been altogether disinterested, but her advice prevailed, and the dawn of the following morning found me in a boat on the unruffled surface of Lough Gill. Arrived at the head of that splendid sheet of water, covered with rich and wooded islands, with their ruined buildings, and bounded by towering mountains, noble plantations, grassy slopes, and precipitous rocks, which give beauty, and, in some places, sublimity to its shores, I proceeded at once up the wide river which forms its principal tributary. The "ould abbey" is chiefly remarkable for having been built at a period nearer to the Reformation than any other ecclesiastical edifice of the same class. Full within view of it, and at the distance of half a mile, stands the shattered remnant of Breffni's princely hall. I strode forward with the enthusiasm of an antiquary, and the high beating heart of a patriotic Irishman. I felt myself on classic ground, immortalized by the lays of Swift and of Moore. I pushed my way into the hallowed precincts of the grand and venerable edifice. I entered its chambers, and, oh my countrymen, I found them converted into the domicile of pigs, cows, and poultry! But the exterior of "O'Rourke's old hall," grey, frowning, and ivy-covered, is well enough; it stands on a beetling precipice, round which a noble river wheels its course. The opposite bank is a very steep ascent, thickly wooded, and rising to a height of at least seventy feet, and, for a quarter of a mile, this beautiful copse follows the course of the river.

The first individual I encountered was an old cowherd; nor was I unfortunate in my Cicerone, for he assured me there were plenty of old stories about strange things that used to be in the place; "but," continued he, "for my own share, I never met any thing worse nor myself. If it bees ould stories that your honour's after, the story about Linn-na-Payshtha and Poul-maw-Gullyawn is the only thing about this place that 's worth one jack-straw. Does your honour see that great big black hole in the river yonder below?" He pointed my attention to a part of the river about fifty yards from the old hall, where a long island occupied the centre of the wide current, the water at one side running shallow, and at the other assuming every appearance of unfathomable depth. The spacious pool, dark and still, wore a death-like quietude of surface. It looked as if the speckled trout would shun its murky precincts—as if even the daring pike would shrink from so gloomy a dwelling-place. "That's Linn-na-Payshtha, sir," resumed my guide, "and Poul-maw-Gullyawn is just the very *moral* of it, only that it's round, and not in a river, but standing out in the middle of a green field, about a short quarter of a mile from this. Well, 'tis as good as fourscore years—I often *hard* my father, God be merciful to him! tell the story—since Manus O'Rourke, a great buckeen, a cock-fighting, drinking blackguard that was long ago, went to sleep one night and had a dream about Linn-na-Payshtha. This Manus, the dirty spalpeen, there, was no ho with him; he thought to ride rough-shod over his betters through the whole country, though he was not one of the real stock of the O'Rourkes. Well, this fellow had a dream that if he dived in Linn-na-Payshtha at twelve o'clock of a Hollow-eve night, he'd find more gold than would make a man of him and his wife while grass grew or water ran. The next night he had the same dream, and sure enough if he had it the second night, it came to him the third in the same form. Manus, well becomes him, never told man-kind or womankind, but swore to himself, by all the books that ever were shut or open, that any how, he would go to the bottom of the big hole. What did he care for the Payshtha-more that was lying there to keep guard on the gold and silver of the old ancient family that was buried there in the wars, packed up in the brewing-pan? Sure he was as good an O'Rourke as the best of them, taking care to forget that his grandmother's father was a cow-boy to the earl O'Donnel. At long last Hollow-eve came, and sly and silent master Manus creeps to bed early, and just at midnight steals down to the river side. When he came to the bank his mind misgave him, and he wheeled up to Frank M'Clure's—the old Frank that was then at that time—and got a bottle of whiskey, and took it with him, and 'tis unknown how much of it he drank. He walked across to the island, and down he went gallantly to the bottom like a stone. Sure enough the Payshtha was there *afore* him, lying like a great big conger eel, seven yards long, and as thick as a bull in the body, with a mane upon his neck like a horse. The Payshtha-more reared himself up, and looking at the poor man as if he'd eat him, says he, in good English,

"'Arrah, then, Manus,' says he, 'what brought you here? It would have been better for you to have blown your brains out at once with a pistol, and have made a quiet end of yourself, than to have come down here for me to deal with you.'

"'Oh, *plase* your honour,' says Manus, 'I beg my life:' and there he stood shaking like a dog in a wet sack.

"'Well, as you have some blood of the O'Rourkes in you, I forgive you this once; but by this, and by that, if ever I see you, or any one belonging to you, coming about this place again, I'll hang a quarter of you on every tree in the wood.'

"'Go home,' says the Payshtha—'go home, Manus,' says he; 'and if you can't make better use of your time, get drunk, but don't come here, bothering me. Yet, stop! since you are here, and have ventured to come, I'll show you something that you'll remember till you go to your grave, and ever after, while you live.'

"With that, my dear, he opens an iron door in the bed of the river, and never the drop of water ran into it; and there Manus sees a long dry cave, or under-ground cellar like, and the Payshtha drags him in, and shuts the door. It wasn't long before the *baste* began to get smaller, and smaller, and smaller; and at last he grew as little as a taughn of twelve years old; and there he was, a brownish little man, about four feet high."

" '*Plase* your honour,' says Manus, 'if I might make so bold, maybe you are one of the good people?'

" 'Maybe I am, and maybe I am not; but, anyhow, all you have to understand is this, that I'm bound to look after the Thiernas* of Breffni, and take care of them through every generation; and that my present business is to watch this cave, and what's in it, till the old stock is reigning over this country once more.'

" 'Maybe you are a sort of a banshee?'

" 'I am not, you fool,' said the little man. 'The banshee is a woman. My business is to live in the form you first saw me in, guarding this spot. And now hold your tongue, and look about you.'

" Manus rubbed his eyes, and looked right and left, before and behind; and there was the vessels of gold and the vessels of silver, the dishes, and the plates, and the cups, and the punch-bowls, and the tankards: there was the golden mether, too, that every Thierna at his wedding used to drink out of to the kerne in real usquebaugh. There was all the money that ever was saved in the family since they got a grant of this manor, in the days of the Firbolgs, down to the time of

* Or *Tighearna*—a lord. Vide O'BRIEN.

their *outer* ruination. He then brought Manus on with him to where there was arms for three hundred men; and the sword set with diamonds, and the golden helmet of the O'Rourke; and he showed him the staff made out of an elephant's tooth, and set with rubies and gold, that the Thierna used to hold while he sat in his great hall, giving justice and the laws of the Brehons to all his clan. The first room in the cave, ye see, had the money and the plate, the second room had the arms, and the third had the books, papers, parchments, title-deeds, wills, and every thing else of the sort belonging to the family.

"'And now, Manus,' says the little man, 'ye seen the whole o' this, and go your ways; but never come to this place any more, or allow any one else. I must keep watch and ward till the Sassanach is *druv* out of Ireland, and the Thiernas o' Breffni in their glory again.' The little man then stopped for a while and looked up in Manus' face, and says to him in a great passion, 'Arrah! bad luck to ye, Manus, why don't ye go about your business?'

"'How can I?—sure you must show me the way out,' says Manus, making answer. The little man then pointed forward with his finger.

"'Can't we go out the way we came?' says Manus.

"'No, you must go out at the other end—that 's the rule o' this place. Ye came in at Linn-na-payshtha, and ye must go out at Poul-maw-gullyawn: ye came down like a stone to the bottom of one hole, and ye must spring up like a cork to the top of the other.' With that the little man gave him one *hoise*, and all that Manus remembers was the roar of the water in his ears; and sure enough he was found the next morning, high and dry, fast asleep, with the empty bottle beside him, but far enough from the place he thought he landed, for it was just below yonder on the island that his wife found him. My father, God be merciful to him! heard Manus swear to every word of the story."

The symbolizing genius of antiquity devised different allegorical beings as the guardians of what was hallowed and secret. In Egypt the Sphynges, placed in rows, lined the approach to the temples of the gods, and many critics regard the cherubim of the Hebrews in the same light. But no creature enjoyed a consideration so extended as the dragon, which, throughout the East and Europe, has at every period been regarded as the sentinel over hidden treasures. A dragon watched the golden apples of the Hesperides; a dragon reposes on the buried gold of Scandinavia and Germany; and the Payshtha-more or great worm, in Ireland, protects the wealth of O'Rourke. Of so wide-spread a belief, perhaps the following is the true origin.

"Couvéra ou Paulestya est le dieu des richesses et des trésors cachés, l'ami des souterrains et des esprits qui y résident, le protecteur des cavernes et des grottes, le roi des rois. Il habite la region du nord. Là, dans Alaka, se demeure ordinaire, au centre d'une épaisse forêt, il est environné d'une cour brillante de genies appelés Kinnaras et Yakchas: ces derniers ont la charge de donner ou de retirer, aux mortels, les biens sur lesquels ils viellent incessamment. Quelquefois le dieu leur souverain se tient dans une grotte profonde gardée par des serpens, et défendue, en outre, par l'eau et par le feu; alors nu, et remarquable par l'énormité de son ventre, il veille lui-même sur ses trésors souterrains." Creuzer, Religions de l'Antiquité, traduction de Guigniaut. Paris, 1825, v. i. p. 248.

On which the translator gives the following note: "L'habitation de Couvéra, au nord, dans les montagnes qui donnent l'or et les pierreries, est remarquable; on voit aussi l'origine de cette opinion, si ancienne et si répandue, qui fait garder par des monstres et des esprits les trésors cachés au sein de la terre."

Mr. Owen (son of Dr. Owen Pughe) has kindly communicated to the compiler of this volume the following particulars respecting some treasure, which still lies concealed in North Wales, and of the efforts made and making to recover it. Mr. Owen's letter is dated Nantglyn, May 10, 1827.

"Some short time ago," he writes, "I was applied to by a man, with a view of ascertaining if I could afford him any assistance in his necromantic pursuits. He informed me he had made considerable progress in the rudiments, and was able to cause noises to disturb the rest of any obnoxious person who had displeased him, and to ascertain the purloiners of lost articles almost to infallibility; that his practice in that way was already pretty considerable, and he expected to enjoy a fair portion of business. In truth, he evinced great expertness in casting nativities, and all the horological and astronomical niceties which distinguish the profound science of astrology.

"This application, he observed, was more particularly instigated from the information which his master in the science had given him of a great treasure, which he had unsuccessfully attempted to obtain. Some forty years before, when the natural enthusiasm of youth, and vain confidence in his necromantic acquirements, had induced him to explore the arcana of nature, he had rashly undertaken an adventure which no person had accomplished. In a bordering parish, tradition (*ar lavar gwla,* or the voice of the country) asserts the existence of a chest filled with gold. So great a prize he thought deserved the most strenuous efforts, and he prepared for the undertaking with the most earnest solicitude.

"Fortified with all that science or resolution could

furnish, he went to the district, and it was not long before his art discovered the unobtrusive spot of the gnomic deposit. He found the entrance of a cave—with breathless expectation he explored its intricacies, and at last arrived at its innermost recess: there he perceived a mighty chest, but some mysterious incubus brooded over the prize. Amid a mass of formless mist he discovered what were evidently talons of a most fearful magnitude, well suited to score the hide of the hapless wight whose spell might not be sufficiently potent to lull the vigilance of this modern Argus; a beak of awful curve, and two lurid eyes, whose basilisk influence unnerved all his powers. He thought he perceived it unfold its wings; dread preparatory of an attack; and finding no time was to be lost, he fumbled for the spell which was to render this appalling menace impotent. He found he had searched in the wrong pocket, and nervous trepidation incapacitated him from a proper use of his faculties; his tongue refused to perform its office; and in this cruel dilemma the impatient fiend pounced upon him. He felt its chilling grasp—and, stretched senseless, he saw no more. When the blood again animated his frame, he found himself laid upon the green sward, and every joint racked with the most excruciating torments. 'In this state,' he observed to his pupil, 'I have remained ever since; my limbs have never recovered their proper tone. I could have exemplified to you the manner in which I must have been treated if I had fortunately preserved the clothes I wore at the time: you would have judged some malicious plough-boy had drawn his harrows over me during my swoon. The scratches on my body in such a lapse of time have of course healed, but their marks remain.' 'My opinion is,' remarked the disciple, 'that he ought not to have undertaken the task alone; and although, when the gold is considered, I would encounter the scratch of a demon with the talons of a condor, yet, as it happened to him, a man may, after groping his way through those devious recesses, and coming suddenly, perhaps, in view of the treasure and its guardian, lose his presence of mind and use the wrong incantation. Now I intend, if you, sir, will write the spell very large and plain, so that this imp can have no pretence to disregard it, to insert it in the cleft of a stick as long as a fishing-rod, and taking care to keep it in advance, I will hold it right under his nose, and then we shall see!'"

Mr. Owen adds that the old professor is still alive, and resides on the banks of the Conwy.

Linn na Payshtha signifies the Pool of the Worm. The latter word is correctly written *Béistin*, the diminutive of *biast* or *piasd*, a little beast, which is used for any worm or insect. The application of the term worm to the serpent tribe is very general; indeed the similarity of form naturally led to it. Any one acquainted with the legends of the north must be familiar with Lind-orms, and in those of Germany the Lind-wurm is no unfrequent actor. Dante calls Satan "Il gran Verme;" Milton's Adam reproaches Eve with having lent an ear "to that false worm;" and Shakspeare says, that slander's tongue "outvenoms all the worms of Nile."

The scene of Dean Swift's well known verses of "O'Rourke's noble feast" was the old hall of Dromahair. They were translated from the Irish of Hugh Mac-Gowran of Glengoole in the county of Leitrim, who was a contemporary. The original begins thus:

"Pleαráca na Ruarcaċ a ccuimne uile duine."

"The Revel-rout of the O'Rourkes is in the memory of all men."

FAIRY LEGENDS.

ROCKS AND STONES.

"Forms in silence frown'd,
Shapeless and nameless; and to mine eye
Sometimes they rolled off cloudily,
Wedding themselves with gloom—or grew
Gigantic to my troubled view,
And seemed to gather round me."

BANIM'S CELT'S PARADISE.

ROCKS AND STONES.

THE LEGEND OF CAIRN THIERNA.

FROM the town of Fermoy, famous for the excellence of its bottled ale, you may plainly see the mountain of Cairn Thierna. It is crowned by a great heap of stones, which, as the country people remark, never came there without "a crooked thought and a cross job." Strange it is, that any work of the good old times should be considered one of labour; for round towers then sprung up like mushrooms in one night, and people played marbles with pieces of rock, that can now no more be moved than the hills themselves.

This great pile on the top of Cairn Thierna was caused by the words of an old woman, whose bed still remains—*Labacally*, the hag's bed—not far from the village of Glanworth. She was certainly far wiser than any woman, either old or young, of my immediate acquaintance. Jove defend me, however, from making an envious comparison between ladies; but facts are stubborn things, and the legend will prove my assertion.

T 2

O'Keefe was lord of Fermoy before the Roches came into that part of the country; and he had an only son—never was there seen a finer child: his young face filled with innocent joy was enough to make any heart glad, yet his father looked on his smiles with sorrow, for an old hag had foretold that this boy should be drowned before he grew up to manhood.

Now, although the prophecies of Pastorini were a failure, it is no reason why prophecies should altogether be despised. The art in modern times may be lost, as well as that of making beer out of the mountain heath, which the Danes did to great perfection. But I take it, the malt of Tom Walker is no bad substitute for the one; and if evil prophecies were to come to pass, like the old woman's, in my opinion we are far more comfortable without such knowledge.

"Infant heir of proud Fermoy,
Fear not fields of slaughter;
Storm nor fire fear not, my boy,
But shun the fatal water."

These were the warning words which caused the chief of Fermoy so much unhappiness. His infant son was carefully prevented all approach to the river, and anxious watch was kept over every playful movement. The child grew up in strength and in beauty, and every day became more dear to his father, who hoping to avert the doom, which however was inevitable, prepared to build a castle far removed from the dreaded element.

The top of Cairn Thierna was the place chosen; and the lord's vassals were assembled, and employed in collecting materials for the purpose. Hither came the fated boy; with delight he viewed the laborious work of raising mighty stones from the base to the summit of the mountain until the vast heap which now forms its rugged crest was accumulated. The workmen were about to commence the building, and the boy, who was considered in safety when on the mountain, was allowed to rove about at will. In his case how true are the words of the great dramatist:

—"Put but a little water in a spoon,
And it shall be, as all the ocean,
Enough to stifle such a *being* up."

A vessel which contained a small supply of water, brought there for the use of the workmen, attracted the attention of the child. He saw, with wonder, the glitter of the sunbeams within it; he approached more near to gaze, when a form resembling his own arose before him. He gave a cry of joy and astonishment, and drew back; the image drew back also, and vanished. Again he approached; again the form appeared, expressing in every feature delight corresponding with his own. Eager to welcome the young stranger, he bent over the vessel to press his lips, and losing his balance, the fatal prophecy was accomplished.

The father in despair abandoned the commenced building; and the materials remain a proof of the folly of attempting to avert the course of fate.

The writer hopes no reader will be uncharitable enough to suspect him of wishing to inculcate a belief in predestination: he only follows his brief. But the truth is, the human mind, as may be observed in the vulgar of every country, has, doubtless owing to its weakness, a strong bias to believe in this doctrine. The tragic muse of Greece delighted to pourtray the unavailing struggles of men "bound in the adamantine chain" of destiny; and the effect on our minds, though humbling, is not dispiriting. Over the East fate is dominant: it not only enters into the serious occupations of life, but extends its empire through the realms of fiction; and the reader, were he not now to be supposed familiar with such coincidences, might perhaps be surprised at the similarity between this legend of the Irish peasant and the exquisite tale of Prince Agib, in the Thousand and One Nights.

Cairn Thierna is the scene of a subsequent tale in

this section; and it only appears necessary to add that the Cork and Dublin mail coach road runs under it. Of the Hag's bed, a plate, though not a particularly correct or picturesque representation, is given in the second volume of Dr. Smith's History of Cork. The Irish name (of this huge block of stone supported by smaller stones) is correctly written *Leaba Cailleach.* Of the hag it may be said, as has been wittily remarked of

——"St. Keven,
If hard lying could gain it, he surely gained heaven;
For on rock lay his limb, and rock pillowed his head,
Whenever this good holy saint kept his bed;
And keep it he must, even to his last day,
For I'm sure he could never have thrown it away."

"*Bà cairt a cheann-adhairt*"—a stone bolster—is the usual account given of the self-mortification of Irish saints, while the hags, their predecessors in the island on which their piety has bestowed celebrity, seemed to prefer an entire couch of the same material. These dames, however, possessed the power of pitching their pillows after any one at whom they were displeased. What is somewhat remarkable, the Finnii, who were contemporaries with the Hags, were rather luxurious in their rest, for tradition relates that

"*Barrughal crann, caonnach, agus ùr-luachair.*"
Branches of trees, moss, and green rushes, formed their beds.

THE ROCK OF THE CANDLE.

A FEW miles west of Limerick stands the once formidable castle of Carrigogunnel. Its riven tower and broken archway remain in mournful evidence of the sieges sustained by that city. Time, however, the great soother of all things, has destroyed the painful effect which the view of recent violence produces on the mind. The ivy creeps around the riven tower, concealing its injuries, and upholding it by a tough swathing of stalks. The archway is again united by the long-armed briar which grows across the rent, and the shattered buttresses are decorated with wild flowers, which gaily spring from their crevices and broken places.

Boldly situated on a rock, the ruined walls of Carrigogunnel now form only a romantic feature in the peaceful landscape. Beneath them, on one side, lies the flat marshy ground called Corkass land, which borders the noble river Shannon; on the other side is seen the neat parish church of Kilkeedy, with its glebe-house and surrounding improvements; and at a short distance appear the irregular mud cabins of the little village of Ballybrown, with the venerable trees of Tervoo.

On the rock of Carrigogunnel, before castle was built, or Brien Boro born to build it, dwelt a hag named Grana, who made desolate the surrounding country. She was gigantic in size, and frightful in appearance. Her eyebrows grew into each other with a grim curve, and beneath their matted bristles, deeply sunk in her head, two small grey eyes darted forth baneful looks of evil. From her deeply wrinkled forehead issued forth a hooked beak, dividing two shrivelled cheeks. Her skinny lips curled with a cruel and malignant expression, and her prominent chin was studded with bunches of grizzly hair.

Death was her sport. Like the angler with his rod, the hag Grana would toil and watch, nor think it labour, so that the death of a victim rewarded her vigils. Every evening did she light an enchanted candle upon the rock, and whoever looked upon it, died before the next morning's sun arose. Numberless were the victims over which Grana rejoiced; one after the other had seen the light, and their death was the consequence. Hence came the country around to be desolate, and Carrigogunnel, the Rock of the Candle, by its dreaded name.

These were fearful times to live in. But the

Finnii of Erin were the avengers of the oppressed. Their fame had gone forth to distant shores, and their deeds were sung by an hundred bards. To them the name of danger was as an invitation to a rich banquet. The web of enchantment stopped their course as little as the swords of an enemy. Many a mother of a son—many a wife of a husband—many a sister of a brother had the valour of the Finnian heroes bereft. Dismembered limbs quivered, and heads bounded on the ground before their progress in battle. They rushed forward with the strength of the furious wind, tearing up the trees of the forest by their roots. Loud was their war-cry as the thunder, raging was their impetuosity above that of common men, and fierce was their anger as the stormy waves of the ocean!

It was the mighty Finn himself who lifted up his voice, and commanded the fatal candle of the hag Grana to be extinguished. "Thine, Regan, be the task," he said, and to him he gave a cap thrice charmed by the magician Luno of Lochlin.

With the star of the same evening the candle of death burned on the rock, and Regan stood beneath it. Had he beheld the slightest glimmer of its blaze, he, too, would have perished, and the hag Grana, with the morning's dawn, rejoiced over his corse. When Regan looked towards the light, the charmed cap fell over his eyes and prevented his seeing. The rock was steep, but he climbed up its craggy side with such caution and dexterity, that, before the hag was aware, the warrior, with averted head, had seized the candle, and flung it with prodigious force into the river Shannon; the hissing waters of which quenched its light for ever!

Then flew the charmed cap from the eyes of Regan, and he beheld the enraged hag with outstretched arms, prepared to seize and whirl him after her candle. Regan instantly bounded westward from the rock just two miles, with a wild and wonderous spring. Grana looked for a moment at the leap, and then tearing up a huge fragment of the rock, flung it after Regan with such tremendous force, that her crooked hands trembled and her broad chest heaved with heavy puffs, like a smith's labouring bellows, from the exertion.

The ponderous stone fell harmless to the ground, for the leap of Regan far exceeded the strength of the furious hag. In triumph he returned to Finn;

"The hero valiant, renowned, and learned;
White-tooth'd, graceful, magnanimous, and active *."

* "An miliḋ armaċ ainmneaċ eolaċ;
Deudġeal, dealbṫaċ, meanmnaċ treoraċ."

The hag Grana was never heard of more; but the stone remains, and, deeply imprinted in it, is still to be seen the mark of the hag's fingers. That stone is far taller than the tallest man, and the power of forty men would fail to move it from the spot where it fell.

The grass may wither around it, the spade and plough destroy dull heaps of earth, the walls of castles fall and perish, but the fame of the Finnii of Erin endures with the rocks themselves, and *Clough-a-Regaun* is a monument fitting to preserve the memory of the deed!

The Finnii are, in Ireland, what the race who fought at Thebes and Troy were in Greece; Sigurd and his companions in Scandinavia; Dictrich and his warriors in Germany; Arthur and his knights in Britain; and Charlemagne and the Paladins in France; that is, mythic heroes, conceived to have far exceeded in strength and prowess the puny beings who now occupy their place. Their deeds were confined to no one part of the island, for hills, rocks, and stones in each province still testify their superhuman might, and many an extant poem and many a traditionary tale record their exploits. The preceding is one of the latter, in which the writer has ventured to retain much of the idiomatic peculiarities of the Irish original.

Regan's leap and the hag's stone-cast will find numerous parallels in the legends of other countries. In German tradition, a young giantess makes a grand clearance of a wide valley; and pitching rocks across an arm of the sea, by way of trying each other's might, was a common amusement of the northern giants.

An humorous friend writes thus of a large stone near Dublin, after describing the various objects which antiquaries had assigned for its use.

" Or left by the giants of old who play'd quoits
When their game they forsook to attack the *potates*.
Potates! sure the root was not then in its glory.
No matter—'tis true as of giants the story!"

CLOUGH NA CUDDY.

Above all the islands in the lakes of Killarney give me Innisfallen—"sweet Innisfallen," as the melodious Moore calls it. It is, in truth, a fairy isle, although I have no fairy story to tell you about it; and if I had, these are such unbelieving times, and people of late have grown so sceptical, that they only smile at my stories, and doubt them.

However, none will doubt that a monastery once stood upon Innisfallen island, for its ruins may still be seen; neither, that within its walls dwelt certain pious and learned persons called Monks. A very pleasant set of fellows they were, I make not the smallest doubt; and I am sure of this, that they had a very pleasant spot to enjoy themselves in after dinner—the proper time, believe me, and I am no bad judge of such matters, for the enjoyment of a fine prospect.

Out of all the monks you could not pick a better fellow nor a merrier soul than father Cuddy: he sung a good song, he told a good story, and had a jolly, comfortable-looking paunch of his own, that was a credit to any refectory table. He was distinguished above all the rest by the name of "the fat father." Now there are many that will take huff at a name; but father Cuddy had no nonsense of that kind about him; he laughed at it—and well able he was to laugh, for his mouth nearly reached from one ear to the other: his might, in truth, be called an open countenance. As his paunch was no disgrace to his food, neither was his nose to his drink. 'Tis a doubt to me if there were not more carbuncles upon it than ever were seen at the bottom of the lake, which is said to be full of them. His eyes had a right merry twinkle in them, like moonshine dancing on the water; and his cheeks had the roundness and crimson glow of ripe arbutus berries.

"He eat, and drank, and prayed, and slept.—
What then?
He eat, and drank, and prayed, and slept again!"

Such was the tenor of his simple life: but when he prayed, a certain drowsiness would come upon him, which, it must be confessed, never occurred when a well-filled "black-Jack" stood before him. Hence his prayers were short and his draughts were long. The world loved him, and he saw no good reason why he should not in return love its venison and its usquebaugh. But, as times went, he must have been a pious man, or else what befel him never would have happened.

Spiritual affairs—for it was respecting the importation of a tun of wine into the island monastery—demanded the presence of one of the brotherhood of Innisfallen at the abbey of Irelagh, now called Mucruss. The superintendence of this important matter was committed to father Cuddy, who felt too deeply interested in the future welfare of any community of which he was a member, to neglect or delay such mission. With the morning's light he was seen guiding his shallop across the crimson waters of the lake towards the peninsula of Mucruss; and having moored his little bark in safety beneath the shelter of a waveworn rock, he advanced with becoming dignity towards the abbey.

The stillness of the bright and balmy hour was broken by the heavy footsteps of the zealous father. At the sound the startled deer, shaking the dew from their sides, sprung up from their lair, and as they bounded off—"Hah!" exclaimed Cuddy, "what a noble haunch goes there!—how delicious it would look smoking upon a goodly platter!"

As he proceeded, the mountain bee hummed his tune of gladness around the holy man, save when buried in the fox-glove bell, or revelling upon a fragrant bunch of thyme; and even then the little voice murmured out happiness in low and broken tones of voluptuous delight. Father Cuddy derived no small comfort from the sound, for it presaged a good metheglin season, and metheglin he regarded, if well manufactured, to be no bad liquor, particularly when there was no stint of usquebaugh in the brewing.

Arrived within the abbey garth, he was received with due respect by the brethren of Irelagh, and arrangements for the embarkation of the wine were completed to his entire satisfaction. "Welcome, father Cuddy," said the prior: "grace be on you."

"Grace before meat, then," said Cuddy, "for a long walk always makes me hungry, and I am certain I have not walked less than half a mile this morning, to say nothing of crossing the water."

A pasty of choice flavour felt the truth of this assertion, as regarded father Cuddy's appetite. After such consoling repast, it would have been a reflection on monastic hospitality to depart without partaking of the grace-cup; moreover, father Cuddy had a particular respect for the antiquity of that custom. He liked the taste of the grace-cup well;—he tried another,—it was no less excellent; and when he had swallowed the third he found his heart expand, and put forth its fibres, willing to embrace all mankind. Surely, then, there is christian love and charity in wine!

I said he sung a good song. Now though psalms are good songs, and in accordance with his vocation, I did not mean to imply that he was a mere psalm-singer. It was well known to the brethren, that wherever father Cuddy was, mirth and melody were with him;—mirth in his eye, and melody on his tongue; and these, from experience, are equally well known to be thirsty commodities; but he took good care never to let them run dry. To please the brotherhood, whose excellent wine pleased him, he sung, and as "*in vino veritas*," his song will well become this veritable history.

"Quam pulchra sunt ova
Cum alba et nova
In stabulo scite leguntur;
Et a Margery bella,
Quæ festiva puella!
Pinguis lardi cum frustis coquuntur.

"Ut belles in prato
Aprico et lato
Sub sole tam læte renident

Ova tosta in mensa,
Mappa bene extensa
Nitidissima lance consident *."

Such was his song. Father Cuddy smacked his lips at the recollection of Margery's delicious fried eggs, which always imparted a peculiar relish to his liquor. The very idea provoked Cuddy to raise the cup to his mouth, and with one hearty pull thereat he finished its contents.

This is, and ever was, a censorious world, often construing what is only a fair allowance into an excess; but I scorn to reckon up any man's drink, like an unrelenting host, therefore I cannot tell how many brimming draughts of wine, bedecked with *the venerable Bead,* father Cuddy emptied

---

* O 'tis eggs are a treat
When so white and so sweet
From under the manger they 're taken,
And by fair Margery,
Och! 'tis she 's full of glee,
They are fried with fat rashers of bacon.

Just like daisies all spread
O'er a broad sunny mead
In the sunbeams so beauteously shining,
Are fried eggs, well display'd
On a dish, when we 've laid
The cloth, and are thinking of dining.

into his "soul-case," so he figuratively termed the body.

His respect for the goodly company of the monks of Irelagh detained him until their adjournment to vespers, when he set forward on his return to Innisfallen. Whether his mind was occupied in philosophic contemplation or wrapped in pious musings, I cannot declare, but the honest father wandered on in a different direction from that in which his shallop lay. Far be it from me to insinuate that the good liquor which he had so commended caused him to forget his road, or that his track was irregular and unsteady. Oh no!—he carried his drink bravely, as became a decent man and a good christian; yet, somehow, he thought he could distinguish two moons. "Bless my eyes," said father Cuddy, "every thing is changing now-a-days!—the very stars are not in the same places they used to be; I think *Camcéachta* (the Plough) is driving on at a rate I never saw it before to-night; but I suppose the driver is drunk, for there are blackguards every where."

Cuddy had scarcely uttered these words, when he saw, or fancied he saw, the form of a young woman, who, holding up a bottle, beckoned him towards her. The night was extremely beautiful, and the white dress of the girl floated gracefully in the moonlight as with gay step she tripped on before the worthy father, archly looking back upon him over her shoulder.

"Ah, Margery, merry Margery!" cried Cuddy, "you tempting little rogue!

'Et a Margery bella,
Quæ festiva puella!'

I see you, I see you and the bottle! let me but catch you, Margery *bella!*" and on he followed, panting and smiling, after this alluring apparition.

At length his feet grew weary, and his breath failed, which obliged him to give up the chase; yet such was his piety that, unwilling to rest in any attitude but that of prayer, down dropped father Cuddy on his knees. Sleep, as usual, stole upon his devotions, and the morning was far advanced when he awoke from dreams, in which tables groaned beneath their load of viands, and wine poured itself free and sparkling as the mountain spring.

Rubbing his eyes, he looked about him, and the more he looked the more he wondered at the alteration which appeared in the face of the country. "Bless my soul and body!" said the good father, "I saw the stars changing last night, but here is a change!" Doubting his senses, he looked again. The hills bore the same majestic outline as on the preceding day, and the lake spread itself beneath his view in the same tranquil beauty, and studded with the same number of islands; but every smaller feature in the landscape was strangely altered. What had been naked rocks, were now clothed with holly and arbutus. Whole woods had disappeared, and waste places had become cultivated fields; and, to complete the work of enchantment, the very season itself seemed changed. In the rosy dawn of a summer's morning he had left the monastery of Innisfallen, and he now felt in every sight and sound the dreariness of winter. The hard ground was covered with withered leaves; icicles depended from leafless branches; he heard the sweet low note of the Robin, who familiarly approached him; and he felt his fingers numbed from the nipping frost. Father Cuddy found it rather difficult to account for such sudden transformations, and to convince himself it was not the illusion of a dream, he was about to arise, when, lo! he discovered both his knees buried at least six inches in the solid stone; for, notwithstanding all these changes, he had never altered his devout position.

Cuddy was now wide awake, and felt, when he got up, his joints sadly cramped, which it was only natural they should be, considering the hard texture of the stone, and the depth his knees had sunk into it. But the great difficulty was to explain how, in one night, summer had become winter, whole woods had been cut down, and well-grown trees had sprouted up. The miracle, nothing else could he conclude it to be, urged him to hasten his return to Innisfallen, where he might learn some explanation of these marvellous events.

Seeing a boat moored within reach of the shore, he delayed not, in the midst of such wonders, to seek his own bark, but, seizing the oars, pulled stoutly towards the island; and here new wonders awaited him.

Father Cuddy waddled, as fast as cramped limbs could carry his rotund corporation, to the gate of the monastery, where he loudly demanded admittance.

"Holloa! whence come you, master monk, and what's your business?" demanded a stranger who occupied the porter's place.

"Business!—my business!" repeated the confounded Cuddy,—"why, do you not know me?" Has the wine arrived safely?"

"Hence, fellow!" said the porter's representative, in a surly tone; "nor think to impose on me with your monkish tales."

"Fellow!" exclaimed the father: "mercy upon us, that I should be so spoken to at the gate of my own house!—Scoundrel!" cried Cuddy, raising his voice, "do you not see my garb—my holy garb?"

"Ay, fellow," replied he of the keys—"the garb of laziness and filthy debauchery, which has been expelled from out these walls. Know you not, idle knave, of the suppression of this nest of superstition, and that the abbey lands and possessions were granted in August last to Master Robert Collan, by our Lady Elizabeth, sovereign queen of England, and paragon of all beauty—whom God preserve!"

"Queen of England!" said Cuddy; "there never was a sovereign queen of England—this is but a piece with the rest. I saw how it was going with the stars last night—the world's turned upside down. But surely this is Innisfallen island, and I am the Father Cuddy who yesterday morning went over to the abbey of Irelagh, respecting the tun of wine. Do you not know me now?"

"Know you!—how should I know you?" said the keeper of the abbey. "Yet true it is, that I have heard my grandmother, whose mother remembered the man, often speak of the fat Father Cuddy of Innisfallen, who made a profane and godless ballad in praise of fried eggs, of which he and his vile crew knew more than they did of the word of God; and who, being drunk, it is said tumbled into the lake one night, and was drowned; but that must have been a hundred, ay, more than a hundred years since."

"'Twas I who composed that song in praise of Margery's fried eggs, which is no profane and godless ballad—no other Father Cuddy than myself ever belonged to Innisfallen," earnestly exclaimed the holy man. "A hundred years!—what was your great-grandmother's name?"

"She was a Mahony of Dunlow—Margaret ni Mahony; and my grandmother—"

"What! merry Margery of Dunlow your great-grandmother!" shouted Cuddy. St. Brandon help me!—the wicked wench, with that tempting bottle! —why, 'twas only last night—a hundred years!—your great-grandmother, said you?—God bless us! there has been a strange torpor over me; I must have slept all this time!"

That Father Cuddy had done so, I think is sufficiently proved by the changes which occurred during his nap. A reformation, and a serious one it was for him, had taken place. Eggs fried by the pretty Margery were no longer to be had in Innisfallen; and, with a heart as heavy as his footsteps, the worthy man directed his course towards Dingle, where he embarked in a vessel on the point of sailing for Malaga. The rich wine of that place had of old impressed him with a high respect for its monastic establishments, in one of which he quietly wore out the remainder of his days.

The stone impressed with the mark of Father Cuddy's knees may be seen to this day. Should any incredulous persons doubt my story, I request them to go to Killarney, where Clough na Cuddy —so is the stone called—remains in Lord Kenmare's park, an indisputable evidence of the fact. Spillane, the bugle-man, will be able to point it out to them, as he did so to me.

Stories of wonderful sleepers are common to most countries; of persons who, having fallen into a slumber, remained so for a long course of years; and who found, on waking, every thing with which they had been familiar altered; all their former friends and companions consigned to the tomb, and a new generation, with new manners and new ideas, arisen in their places. It was thus that Greece fabled of Epimenides, the epic poet of Crete, who, going in search of one of his sheep, entered a cavern to repose during the mid-day heat, and slept there quietly, according to Eudamus, for forty-seven years, while Pausanias states his nap to have extended thirty years more. When he awoke, fancying that he had only taken a short doze, he proceeded in quest of his ewe.

The legend of the Seven Sleepers was current throughout the East, since the Prophet has deigned to give them a place in the Koran. Their story, the most famous one of the kind, will be found in the *Mines de l'Orient,* where it is related at great length.

The scene of a similar legend is placed by Paulus Diaconus on the shore of the Baltic, where, in "a darke and obscure caverne," five men were found sleeping, "their bodies and garments in no part consumed, but sound and whole as at first, who by their habits appeared to be ancient Romans. Certaine of the inhabitants had often made attempts to waken them, but could not. Upon a time, a wicked fellow purposing to dispoile and rob one of them of his garment, he no sooner touched it but his hand withered and dried up. Olaus Magnus was of opinion that they were confined thither to some strange purpose, that when their trance was expired they might either discover strange visions revealed unto them, or else they were to teach and preach the christian faith to infidels, who never knew the evangelicall doctrine." *Heywood's Hierarchie of the Blessed Angells.*

In German tradition we meet the account of the woman who sought a night's lodging from the celebrated Heïling, and who, when she awoke in the morning, found herself lying at the foot of a rock, where she had slept an hundred years: and also the tale of honest Peter Klaus, who slumbered for twenty years in the bowling-green of Kyffhäuser; which last has furnished Mr. Washington Irving with the groundwork of his incomparable Rip van Winkle; a beautiful specimen of the mode in which true genius is able to borrow and appropriate.

Another sleepy legend, related in Ireland, called "the Song of the little Bird," was communicated to the Amulet, for 1827, one of the elegant literary toys which make their annual appearance.

Miss Luby, in her poem on Killarney, has preserved the story of Clough na Cuddy, both in clever verse and in a prose note. The localities mentioned will be perfectly familiar to all who have visited that region of enchantment. Part of the monastic ruins on Innisfallen have been converted into a banqueting-house, which is the subject of the vignette title-page of Mr. Weld's account of those lakes; a work worthy of the scenery it illustrates.

Mr. Moore has written some exquisite verses, in the Irish Melodies, on his departure from that island; and a sonnet and two-thirds, of a less sentimental nature, on dining there, was extracted from an artist's sketch-book. These lines may be quoted in support of the legend, as evidence of the reputed character of the pious chroniclers of Innisfallen; but as "in vino veritas," their work, if not the very best, is certainly one of the best, Irish historical records extant.

"Hail, reverend fathers! whose long-buried bones
Still sanctify this sod whereon we dine,
And take, as we are wont, our glass of wine.
Behold, we pour, amid these hallow'd stones,

Libation due, unto your thirsty clay!
For to be dry for now six hundred years,
Upon my soul, good fathers! moves my tears,
And almost makes me rather drink than pray,
To think of what a long long thirst you have;
You who were wet and merry souls, I wot,
And most ecclesiastically took your pot.
'Tis pity, faith it is, you 're in the grave:
But since it is our common fate, alas!
Good by, good friars!—Come, Tom, fill your glass.

Quoth Thomas, gravely, 'I do much revere
The clay wherein such reverend bones do lie;
Yet thus to toast them, I would not comply,
But that their reverences are where they are;
For were they face to face, God bless my soul!
And we had twice as many jugs and bottles,
And they set to, with all their thirsty throttles,
A pretty hearing we 'd have of our bowl.'"

BARRY OF CAIRN THIERNA.

FERMOY, though now so pretty and so clean a town, was once as poor and as dirty a village as any in Ireland. It had neither great barracks, grand church, nor buzzing schools. Two-storied houses were but few: its street—for it had but one—was chiefly formed of miserable mud cabins; nor was the fine scenery around sufficient to induce the traveller to tarry in its paltry inn beyond the limits actually required.

In those days it happened that a regiment of foot was proceeding from Dublin to Cork. One company, which left Caher in the morning, had, with "toilsome march," passed through Mitchelstown, tramped across the Kilworth mountains, and, late of an October evening, tired and hungry, reached Fermoy, the last stage but one of their quarters. No barracks were then built there to receive them; and every voice was raised, calling to the gaping villagers for the name and residence of the billet-master.

"Why, then, can't you be easy now, and let a

body tell you," said one. "Sure, then, how can I answer you all at once?" said another. "Anan!" cried a third, affecting not to understand the serjeant who addressed him. "Is it Mr. Consadine you want?" replied a fourth, answering one question by asking another. "Bad luck to the whole breed of *sogers!*" muttered a fifth villager—"it's come to eat poor people that work for their bread out of house and home you are." "Whisht, Teigue, can't you now?" said his neighbour, jogging the last speaker; "there's the house, gentlemen—you see it there yonder forenent you, at the bottom of the street, with the light in the window; or stay, myself would think little of running down with you, poor creatures! for 'tis tired and weary you must be after the road." "That's an honest fellow," said several of the dust-covered soldiers; and away scampered Ned Flynn, with all the men of war following close at his heels.

Mr. Consadine, the billet-master was, as may be supposed, a person of some, and on such occasions as the present, of great consideration in Fermoy. He was of a portly build, and of a grave and slow movement, suited at once to his importance and his size. Three inches of fair linen were at all times visible between his waistband and waistcoat. His breeches-pockets were never buttoned; and, scorning to conceal the bull-like proportions of his chest and neck, his collar was generally open, as he wore no cravat. A flaxen bob-wig commonly sat fairly on his head and squarely on his forehead, and an *ex-officio* pen was stuck behind his ear. Such was Mr. Consadine: billet-master-general, barony sub-constable, and deputy-clerk of the sessions, who was now just getting near the end of his eighth tumbler in company with the proctor, who at that moment had begun to talk of coming to something like a fair settlement about his tithes, when Ned Flynn knocked.

"See who's at the door, Nelly," said the eldest Miss Consadine, raising her voice, and calling to the barefooted servant girl.

"'Tis the *sogers*, sir, is come!" cried Nelly, running back into the room without opening the door; "I hear the *jinketing* of their swords and *bagnets* on the paving stones."

"Never welcome them at this hour of the night," said Mr. Consadine, taking up the candle, and moving off to the room on the opposite side of the hall which served him for an office.

Mr. Consadine's own pen and that of his son Tom were now in full employment. The officers were sent to the inn; the serjeants, corporals, &c. were billeted on those who were on indifferent terms with Mr. Consadine; for, like a worthy man, he leaned as light as he could on his friends.

The soldiers had nearly all departed for their quarters, when one poor fellow, who had fallen asleep, leaning on his musket against the wall, was awakened by the silence, and, starting up, he went over to the table at which Mr. Consadine was seated, hoping his worship would give him a good billet.

"A good billet, my lad," said the billet-master-general, barony sub-constable, and deputy-clerk of the sessions—"that you shall have, and on the biggest house in the place. Do you hear, Tom! make out a billet for this man upon Mr. Barry of Cairn Thierna."

"On Mr. Barry of Cairn Thierna!" said Tom with surprise.

"Yes; on Mr. Barry of Cairn Thierna—the great Barry!" replied his father giving a nod, and closing his right eye slowly, with a semi-drunken wink. "Is not he said to keep the grandest house in this part of the country?—or stay, Tom, just hand me over the paper, and I'll write the billet myself."

The billet was made out accordingly; the sand glittered on the signature and broad flourishes of Mr. Consadine, and the weary grenadier received it with becoming gratitude and thanks. Taking up his knapsack and firelock he left the office, and Mr. Consadine waddled back to the proctor to chuckle over the trick that he played the soldier, and to laugh at the idea of his search after Barry of Cairn Thierna's house.

Truly had he said no house could vie in capacity with Mr. Barry's; for, like Allan-a-Dale's, its roof was

> "The blue vault of heaven, with its crescent so
> pale."

Barry of Cairn Thierna was one of the chieftains who, of old, lorded it over the barony of Barry-more, and for some reason or other he had become enchanted on the mountain of Cairn Thierna, where he was known to live in great state, and was often seen by the belated peasant.

Mr. Consadine had informed the soldier that Mr. Barry lived a little way out of the town, on the Cork road; so the poor fellow trudged along for some time, with eyes right and eyes left, looking for the great house; but nothing could he see, only the dark mountain of Cairn Thierna before him, and an odd cabin or two on the road side. At last he met a man, of whom he asked the way to Mr. Barry's.

"To Mr. Barry's!" said the man; "what Barry is it you want?"

"I can't say exactly in the dark," returned the soldier. "Mr. What's-his-name, the billet master, has given me the direction on my billet; but he said it was a large house, and I think he called him the great Mr. Barry."

"Why, sure, it wouldn't be the great Barry of Cairn Thierna you are asking about?"

"Ay," said the soldier, "Cairn Thierna—that's the very place: can you tell me where it is?"

"Cairn Thierna," repeated the man; "Barry of Cairn Thierna—I 'll show you the way and welcome; but it 's the first time in all my born days that ever I heard of a soldier being billeted on Barry of Cairn Thierna. 'Tis surely a queer thing for old Dick Consadine to be after sending you there," continued he; "but you see that big mountain before you—that 's Cairn Thierna. Any one will show you Mr. Barry's when you get to the top of it, up to the big heap of stones."

The weary soldier gave a sigh as he walked forward towards the mountain; but he had not proceeded far when he heard the clatter of a horse coming along the road after him, and turning his head round, he saw a dark figure rapidly approaching him. A tall gentleman, richly dressed, and mounted on a noble gray horse, was soon at his side, when the rider pulled up, and the soldier repeated his inquiry after Mr. Barry's of Cairn Thierna.

"I'm Barry of Cairn Thierna," said the gentleman; "what is your business with me, friend?"

"I've got a billet on your house, sir," replied the soldier, from the billet-master of Fermoy."

"Have you, indeed?" said Mr. Barry; "well, then, it is not very far off; follow me, and you shall be well taken care of."

He turned off the road, and led his horse up the steep side of the mountain, followed by the soldier, who was astonished at seeing the horse proceed with so little difficulty, where he was obliged to scramble up, and could hardly find or keep his footing. When they got to the top there was a house sure enough, far beyond any house in Fermoy. It was three stories high, with fine windows, and all lighted up within, as if it was full of grand company. There was a hall door, too, with a flight of stone steps before it, at which Mr. Barry dismounted, and the door was opened to him by a servant man, who took his horse round to the stable.

Mr. Barry, as he stood at the door, desired the soldier to walk in, and instead of sending him down to the kitchen, as any other gentleman would have done, brought him into the parlour, and desired to see his billet.

"Ay," said Mr. Barry, looking at it and smiling,

"I know Dick Consadine well—he's a merry fellow, and has got some excellent cows on the inch field of Carrickabrick; a sirloin of good beef is no bad thing for supper.

Mr. Barry then called out to some of his attendants, and desired them to lay the cloth, and make all ready, which was no sooner done than a smoking sirloin of beef was placed before them.

"Sit down, now, my honest fellow," said Mr. Barry, "you must be hungry after your long day's march."

The soldier, with a profusion of thanks for such hospitality, and acknowledgments for such condescension, sat down, and made, as might be expected, an excellent supper; Mr. Barry never letting his jaws rest for want of helping until he was fairly done. Then the boiling water was brought in, and such a jug of whiskey punch was made, there was no faulting it.

They sat together a long time, talking over the punch, and the fire was so good, and Mr. Barry himself was so good a gentleman, and had such fine converse about every thing in the world, far or near, that the soldier never felt the night going over him. At last Mr. Barry stood up, saying, it was a rule with him that every one in his house should be in bed by twelve o'clock, "and," said he, pointing to a bundle which lay in one corner of the room, "take that to bed with you, it's the hide of the cow which I had killed for your supper; give it to the billet-master when you go back to Fermoy in the morning, and tell him that Barry of Cairn Thierna sent it to him. He will soon understand what it means, I promise you; so good night, my brave fellow; I wish you a comfortable sleep, and every good fortune; but I must be off and away out of this long before you are stirring."

The soldier gratefully returned his host's good night and good wishes, and went off to the room which was shown him, without claiming, as every one knows he had a right to do, the second-best bed in the house.

Next morning the sun awoke him. He was lying on the broad of his back, and the sky-lark was singing over him in the beautiful blue sky, and the bee was humming close to his ear among the heath. He rubbed his eyes; nothing did he see but the clear sky, with two or three light morning clouds floating away. Mr. Barry's fine house and soft feather bed had melted into air, and he found himself stretched on the side of Cairn Thierna, buried in the heath, with the cow-hide which had been given him rolled up under his head for a pillow.

"Well," said he, "this beats cock-fighting! —Didn't I spend the pleasantest night I ever spent in my life with Mr. Barry last night?—

And what in the world has become of the house, and the hall door with the steps, and the very bed that was under me?"

He stood up. Not a vestige of a house or any thing like one, but the rude heap of stones on the top of the mountain, could he see, and ever so far off lay the Blackwater glittering with the morning sun, and the little quiet village of Fermoy on its banks, from whose chimneys white wreaths of smoke were beginning to rise upwards into the sky.

Throwing the cow-hide over his shoulder, he descended, not without some difficulty, the steep side of the mountain, up which Mr. Barry had led his horse the preceding night with so much ease, and he proceeded along the road, pondering on what had befallen him.

When he reached Fermoy, he went straight to Mr. Consadine's, and asked to see him.

"Well, my gay fellow," said the official Mr. Consadine, recognising, at a glance, the soldier, "what sort of an entertainment did you meet with from Barry of Cairn Thierna?"

"The best of treatment, sir," replied the soldier; "and well did he speak of you, and he desired me to give you this cow-hide as a token to remember him."

"Many thanks to Mr. Barry for his generosity,"

said the billet-master, making a bow in mock solemnity; "many thanks, indeed, and a right good skin it is, wherever he got it."

Mr. Consadine had scarcely finished the sentence when he saw his cow-boy running up the street, shouting and crying aloud that the best cow in the inch field was lost and gone, and nobody knew what had become of her, or could give the least tidings of her.

The soldier had flung the skin on the ground, and the cow-boy looking at it, exclaimed—

"That is her hide, wherever she is!—I 'd take my bible oath to the two small white spots, with the glossy black about them, and there 's the very place where she rubbed the hair off her shoulder last Martinmas." Then clapping his hands together, he literally sung, to "the tune the old cow died of,"

Agus oro Drimen duve; oro bo
Oro Drimen duve; mhiel agrah!
Agus oro Drimen duve—O—Ochone!
Drimen duve deelish—go den tu slane beugh *.

---

* This, which is written as it is pronounced, may be translated—

And oh, my black cow—oh my cow,
Oh my black cow, a thousand times dear to me;
And oh my black cow—alas, alas,
My darling black cow, why did you leave me.

This lamentation was stopped short by Mr. Consadine.

"There is no manner of doubt of it," said he. "It was Barry who killed my best cow, and all he has left me is the hide of the poor beast to comfort myself with; but it will be a warning to Dick Consadine for the rest of his life never again to play off his tricks upon travellers."

An anonymous correspondent before alluded to, has supplied the compiler with the outline of the foregoing tale. Another version, in which a fair dame named Una (Anglicè, Winny, who proves to be the queen of the Fairies) is substituted for Mr. Barry, was related to him some years since, under the title of "the Lady of the Rock." The circumstances of the billet, the supper, the hide, and the billet master's loss of his best cow, are precisely similar in both. The scene of the story was Blarney, and the soldier said to be one of Cromwell's troopers.

According to tradition, the great Barry has his magic dwelling on the summit of Cairn Thierna, the legend of which mountain will be found in the present section. He appears to belong to the same class of beings as Gileroon Doonoch, or Gileroon of the old Head of Kinsale; Farwinneth O'Kilbritaune, or the Green Man of Kilbrittan; Garold Earloch, or Early Garrett of Killarney, &c. respecting whom stories very similar to the foregoing and subsequent are related. These superhuman mortals also commonly appear before any remarkable event, like the German Emperor Charles V., who, with his army, according to tradition, inhabit the Odenberg, in Hesse, and when war is on the eve of breaking out, the mountain opens, the Emperor issues forth, sounds his bugle, and with his host passes over to another mountain. Rodenstein, who in a similar manner announces war, was seen so recently as 1815, previous to the landing of Napoleon, to pass with his followers from Schnelbert to his former strong hold of Rodenstein.

An account of the rise of the town of Fermoy to its present state from the poor village described, may be found in the second volume of Brewer's Beauties of Ireland; a work which will materially assist those inclined to acquire a correct knowledge of that country. Mr. Brewer's character is already well known and highly esteemed, as an accurate observer, a pleasing writer, and a careful and industrious compiler: and judging from the volumes which have appeared, the "Beauties of Ireland" are worthy of that gentleman's reputation.

THE GIANT'S STAIRS.

On the road between Passage and Cork there is an old mansion called Ronayne's Court. It may be easily known from the stack of chimneys and the gable ends, which are to be seen look at it which way you will. Here it was that Maurice Ronayne and his wife Margaret Gould kept house, as may be learned to this day from the great old chimney-piece, on which is carved their arms. They were a mighty worthy couple, and had but one son, who was called Philip, after no less a person than the King of Spain.

Immediately on his smelling the cold air of this world the child sneezed, which was naturally taken to be a good sign of his having a clear head; and the subsequent rapidity of his learning was truly amazing, for on the very first day a primer was put into his hand, he tore out the A, B, C, page, and destroyed it, as a thing quite beneath his notice. No wonder then that both father and mother were proud of their heir, who gave such indisputable proofs of genius, or, as they call it in that part of the world, "*genus.*"

One morning, however, Master Phil, who was then just seven years old, was missing, and no one could tell what had become of him: servants were sent in all directions to seek him, on horseback and on foot, but they returned without any tidings of the boy, whose disappearance altogether was most unaccountable. A large reward was offered, but it produced them no intelligence, and years rolled away without Mr. and Mrs. Ronayne having obtained any satisfactory account of the fate of their lost child.

There lived, at this time, near Carrigaline, one Robert Kelly, a blacksmith by trade. He was what is termed a handy man, and his abilities were held in much estimation by the lads and the lasses of the neighbourhood; for, independent of shoeing horses, which he did to great perfection, and making plough irons, he interpreted dreams for the young women, sung Arthur O'Bradley at their weddings, and was so good natured a fellow at a christening, that he was gossip to half the country round.

Now it happened that Robin had a dream himself, and young Philip Ronayne appeared to him in it at the dead hour of the night. Robin thought he saw the boy mounted upon a beautiful white horse, and that he told him how he was made a page to the giant Mahon Mac Mahon, who had carried him off, and who held his court in the hard heart of the rock. "The seven years—my time of service—are clean out, Robin," said he, "and if you release me this night, I will be the making of you for ever after."

"And how will I know," said Robin—cunning enough, even in his sleep—"but this is all a dream?"

"Take that," said the boy, "for a token"—and at the word the white horse struck out with one of his hind legs, and gave poor Robin such a kick in the forehead, that thinking he was a dead man, he roared as loud as he could after his brains, and woke up calling a thousand murders. He found himself in bed, but he had the mark of the blow, the regular print of a horse-shoe upon his forehead as red as blood; and Robin Kelly, who never before found himself puzzled at the dream of any other person, did not know what to think of his own.

Robin was well acquainted with the Giant's Stairs, as, indeed, who is not that knows the harbour? They consist of great masses of rock, which, piled one above another, rise like a flight of steps, from very deep water, against the bold cliff of Carrigmahon. Nor are they badly suited for stairs to those who have legs of sufficient length to stride over a moderate sized house, or to enable them to clear the space of a mile in a hop, step, and jump. Both these feats the giant Mac Mahon was said to have performed in the days of Finnian glory; and the common tradition of the country placed his dwelling within the cliff up whose side the stairs led.

Such was the impression which the dream made on Robin, that he determined to put its truth to the test. It occurred to him, however, before setting out on this adventure, that a plough iron may be no bad companion, as, from experience, he knew it was an excellent knock-down argument, having, on more occasions than one, settled a little disagreement very quietly: so, putting one on his shoulder, off he marched, in the cool of the evening, through Glaun a Thowk (the Hawk's Glen) to Monkstown. Here an old gossip of his (Tom Clancey by name) lived, who, on hearing Robin's dream, promised him the use of his skiff, and moreover offered to assist in rowing it to the Giant's Stairs.

After a supper which was of the best, they embarked. It was a beautiful still night, and the little boat glided swiftly along. The regular dip of the oars, the distant song of the sailor, and sometimes the voice of a belated traveller at the ferry of Carrigaloe, alone broke the quietness of the land and sea and sky. The tide was in their favour, and in a few minutes Robin and his gossip rested on their oars under the dark shadow of the Giant's Stairs. Robin looked anxiously for the entrance to the Giant's palace, which, it was said, may be found by any one seeking it at midnight; but no such entrance could he see. His impatience had hurried him there before that time, and after waiting a considerable space in a state of suspense not to be described, Robin, with pure vexation, could not help exclaiming to his companion, "'Tis a pair of fools we are, Tom Clancey, for coming here at all on the strength of a dream."

"And whose doing is it," said Tom, "but your own?"

At the moment he spoke they perceived a faint glimmering of light to proceed from the cliff, which gradually increased until a porch big enough for a king's palace unfolded itself almost on a level with the water. They pulled the skiff directly towards the opening, and Robin Kelly seizing his plough iron, boldly entered with a strong hand and a stout heart. Wild and strange was that entrance; the whole of which appeared formed of grim and grotesque faces, blending so strangely each with the other that it was impossible to define any: the chin of one formed the nose of another: what appeared to be a fixed and stern eye, if dwelt upon, changed to a gaping mouth; and the lines of the lofty forehead grew into a majestic and flowing beard. The more Robin allowed himself to contemplate the forms around him, the more terrific they became; and the stony expression of this crowd of faces assumed a savage ferocity as his imagination converted feature after feature into a different shape and character. Losing the twilight in which these indefinite forms were visible, he advanced through a dark and devious passage, whilst a deep and rumbling noise sounded as if the rock was about to close upon him and swallow him up alive for ever. Now, indeed, poor Robin felt afraid.

"Robin, Robin," said he, "if you were a fool for coming here, what in the name of fortune are you now?" But, as before, he had scarcely spoken, when he saw a small light twinkling through the darkness of the distance, like a star in the midnight sky. To retreat was out of the question; for so many turnings and windings were in the passage, that he considered he had but little chance of making his way back. He therefore proceeded towards the bit of light, and came at last into a spacious chamber, from the roof of which hung the solitary lamp that had guided him. Emerging from such profound gloom, the single lamp afforded Robin abundant light to discover several gigantic figures seated round a massive stone table as if in serious deliberation, but no word disturbed the breathless silence which prevailed. At the head of this table sat Mahon Mac Mahon himself, whose majestic beard had taken root, and in the course of ages grown into the stone slab. He was the first who perceived Robin; and instantly starting up, drew his long beard from out the huge piece of rock in such haste and with so sudden a jerk that it was shattered into a thousand pieces.

"What seek you?" he demanded in a voice of thunder.

"I come," answered Robin, with as much boldness as he could put on; for his heart was almost fainting within him—"I come," said he, "to claim Philip Ronayne, whose time of service is out this night."

"And who sent you here?" said the giant.

"'Twas of my own accord I came," said Robin.

"Then you must single him out from among my pages," said the giant; "and if you fix on the wrong one, your life is the forfeit. Follow me." He led Robin into a hall of vast extent, and filled with lights; along either side of which were rows of beautiful children all apparently seven years old, and none beyond that age, dressed in green, and every one exactly dressed alike.

"Here," said Mahon, "you are free to take

Philip Ronayne, if you will; but, remember, I give but one choice."

Robin was sadly perplexed; for there were hundreds upon hundreds of children; and he had no very clear recollection of the boy he sought. But he walked along the hall, by the side of Mahon, as if nothing was the matter, although his great iron dress clanked fearfully at every step, sounding louder than Robin's own sledge battering on his anvil.

They had nearly reached the end without speaking, when Robin seeing that the only means he had was to make friends with the giant, determined to try what effect a few soft words might have.

"'Tis a fine wholesome appearance the poor children carry," remarked Robin, "although they have been here so long shut out from the fresh air and the blessed light of heaven. 'Tis tenderly your honour must have reared them!"

"Ay," said the giant, "that is true for you; so give me your hand; for you are, I believe, a very honest fellow for a blacksmith."

Robin at the first look did not much like the huge size of the hand, and therefore presented his plough-iron, which the giant seizing, twisted in his grasp round and round again as if it had been a potatoe stalk; on seeing this all the children set up a shout of laughter. In the midst of their mirth Robin thought he heard his name called; and all ear and eye, he put his hand on the boy whom he fancied had spoken, crying out at the same time, "Let me live or die for it, but this is young Phil Ronayne."

"It is Philip Ronayne—happy Philip Ronayne," said his young companions; and in an instant the hall became dark. Crashing noises were heard, and all was in strange confusion; but Robin held fast his prize, and found himself lying in the gray dawn of the morning at the head of the Giant's Stairs with the boy clasped in his arms.

Robin had plenty of gossips to spread the story of his wonderful adventure—Passage, Monkstown, Carrigaline—the whole barony of Kerricurrihy rung with it.

"Are you quite sure, Robin, it is young Phil Ronayne you have brought back with you?" was the regular question; for although the boy had been seven years away, his appearance now was just the same as on the day he was missed. He had neither grown taller nor older in look, and he spoke of things which had happened before he was carried off as one awakened from sleep, or as if they had occurred yesterday.

"Am I sure? Well, that's a queer question,"

was Robin's reply; "seeing the boy has the blue eyes of the mother, with the foxy hair of the father; to say nothing of the *purty* wart on the right side of his little nose."

However Robin Kelly may have been questioned, the worthy couple of Ronayne's court doubted not that he was the deliverer of their child from the power of the giant Mac Mahon; and the reward they bestowed on him equalled their gratitude.

Philip Ronayne lived to be an old man; and he was remarkable to the day of his death for his skill in working brass and iron, which it was believed he had learned during his seven years' apprenticeship to the giant Mahon Mac Mahon.

This legend, in some particulars, resembles those told in Wales of Owen Lawgoch, or Owen of the bloody hand: in Denmark, of Holger the Dane: in Germany, of Frederic Barbarosa, or red beard, &c. The writer of a valuable paper in the Quarterly Review has thus condensed the story, which may be found in Mr. Thiele's Danske Folkesagn, &c.

"The emperor (Frederic) is secluded in the castle of Kyffhaüsen, in the Hercynian forest, where he remains in a state not much unlike the description which Cervantes has given of the inhabitants of the cavern of Montesinos: he slumbers on his throne—his red beard has grown through the stone table on which his light arm reclines, or, as some say, it has grown round and round it. A variation of the same fable, coloured according to its locality, is found in Denmark; where it is said, that Holger Danske, whom the French romances call Ogier the Dane, slumbers in the vaults beneath Cronenburgh castle. A villain was once allured by splendid offers to descend into the cavern and visit the half-torpid hero. Ogier muttered to the visitor, requesting him to stretch out his hand. The villain presented an iron crow to Ogier, who grasped it, indenting the metal with his fingers. 'It is well!' quoth Ogier, who imagined he was squeezing the hand of the stranger, and thus provoking his strength and fortitude: 'there are yet *men* in Denmark.'"

Billy Quinn, the poet of Passage, has sung the charms of the scenery of this legend in such popular numbers, that it is presumed the reader will not be displeased at finding a verse here. After praising the noble river Lee, he tells us that at Passage

"A ferry-boat's there, quite convenient
For man and horse to take a ride;
Who, both in clover, may go over
To Carrigaloe at the other side.
'Tis there is seen—oh! the sweet Marino
With trees so green oh, and fruit so red—
Brave White-point, and right forenent it
The Giant's Stairs, and old Horse's head."

The witty Mr. Henry Bennett, in his pleasant local poem of the Steam Boat, is pleased to call the Giant's Stairs

——— "a flight
of fancy."

It may be so: but against such authority the compiler is enabled to support the truth of this legend, at least, by circumstantial evidence. A wonderful pair of cubes have been exhibited to him in proof of Mr. Ronayne's supernatural handicraft. Dr. Smith, in his History of Cork, vol. i. p. 172, also says that "he (Mr. Philip Ronayne) invented a cube which is perforated in such a manner that a second cube *of the same dimensions exactly in all respects* may be passed through the same."

And now, farewell! the fairy dream is o'er:
The tales my infancy had loved to hear,
Like blissful visions, fade and disappear.
Such tales Momonia's peasant tells no more!
Vanish'd are MERMAIDS *from her sea-beat shore;*
Check'd is the HEADLESS HORSEMAN'S *strange career;*
FIR DARRIG'S *voice no longer mocks the ear,*
Nor ROCKS *bear wonderous imprints as of yore!*
Such is "the march of mind."—But did the fays
(Creatures of whim—the gossamers of will)
In Ireland work such sorrow and such ill
As stormier spirits of our modern days?
Oh land beloved! no angry voice I raise;
My constant prayer—"may peace be with thee still."

ERRATA.

Page 101, line 23, for *Folksagn*, read *Folkesagn*.
108, 22, *for* gessoon, *read* gossoon.
111, 22, *for* Græn, *read* Grœn.
129, 18, for *humanos*, read *hermanos*.
137, 12, *for* dares, *read* does.
160, 9, *for* ought, *read* out.
175, 3, *for* Beetham, *read* Betham.
217, 18, for *Keineswegs*, read *Keinesweges*.
233, 6, *for* Sagan, *read* Sagen.

LONDON:
PRINTED BY THOMAS DAVISON, WHITEFRIARS.